GREAT AMERICAN ⟨ FOR JAMES BEARD AND JULIA CHILD, WHO LIT THE LAMP AND SHOWED US THE WAY ⟩ COOKING SCHOOLS

D1568671

GREAT AMERICAN COOKING SCHOOLS

American Food & California Wine
Bountiful Bread: Basics to Brioches
Christmas Feasts from History
Romantic & Classic Cakes
Cooking of the South
Dim Sum & Chinese One-Dish Meals
Fine Fresh Food—Fast
Fresh Garden Vegetables
Ice Cream & Ices
Omelettes & Soufflés
Pasta! Cooking It, Loving It
Quiche & Pâté
Soups & Salads
Successful Parties: Simple & Elegant

Romantic AND Classic Cakes

ROSE LEVY BERANBAUM

ILLUSTRATED BY JANE ROSENBERG

IRENA CHALMERS COOKBOOKS, INC. • **NEW YORK**

For my dear friend and husband, Elliott Beranbaum, and my dear friend Cecily Brownstone. With gratitude to my wonderful family for helping me to have the time and energy to make this book possible.

IRENA CHALMERS COOKBOOKS, INC.

PUBLISHER
Irena Chalmers

Sales and Marketing Director
Diane J. Kidd

Managing Editor
Jean Atcheson

Series Design
Helene Berinsky

Cover Design
Milton Glaser
Karen Skelton, *Associate Designer*

Cover Photography
Georgiana Silk (cake)
Matthew Klein

Editor for this book
Jennifer Sparks

Typesetting
Cosmos Press, New York

Printing
Lucas Litho, Inc., Baltimore

Editorial Offices
23 East 92nd Street
New York, NY 10028
(212) 289-3105

Sales Offices
P.O. Box 322
Brown Summit, NC 27214
(919) 656-3115

ISBN # 0-941034-06-2
© 1981 by Rose Levy Beranbaum. All rights reserved.
Printed and published in the United States of America
by Irena Chalmers Cookbooks, Inc.
LIBRARY OF CONGRESS
CATALOG CARD NO.: 81-68841
  Beranbaum, Rose Levy
    Romantic and classic cakes.

  Greensboro, N.C.: Chalmers, Irena Cookbooks, Inc.
84 p.
8108   810722

Contents

Introduction

My entrance into the food profession came unwittingly at the age of five when, for the first time, I was paid to taste something. In those days food held no charms for me, and to stave off what my grandmother was convinced would be certain starvation, she offered me 10 cents to give her homemade applesauce one more try (I claimed it was not up to my standards because it had lumps in it).

For years, eating was little more than a battle of wills between me and my grandmother and mother. When I was in high school one of my mother's friends told me about Gandhi and his hunger strikes. She regretted this when in the middle of the dinner hour one night I called her to ask exactly how a hunger strike was carried out—did it mean no water as well as food? Sensing what was at stake, she immediately made it clear that Gandhi's hunger strikes were used for the sake of great issues for mankind and not for petty adolescent grievances.

My all-consuming interest in food as a creative endeavor emerged when I started cooking and discovered that it was possible, if one could ever unearth and conquer all the mysteries and secrets, to make things taste and feel the way I wanted them to. After trying for years to make frostings taste like bakery frostings, I finally realized that the reason for my failure was that mine were not the same, they were better. (I was trying to duplicate the fluffy, airy, vegetable-shortening frostings using pure unsalted butter).

In the French culinary hierarchy, the *chefs de cuisine* refer to the pastry makers (*patissiers*) as "those fanatics." The pastry makers have their revenge by calling the candy makers the St. Cyr, or militarists, of the food profession. The candy makers (*confiseurs*), I suppose, are so busy controlling humidity and temperature to prevent "chocolate bloom" that they are above name-calling. There is no doubt that in order to achieve any sort of consistent success in the baking and confection area, a certain measure of near-compulsive exactness is highly desirable. A baker is working with ingredients that are highly susceptible to changes in the environmental conditions. Knowing the rules will prevent needless frustration. Here is an instance where understanding truly sets you free to be creative and innovative. Baking is a science in which many variables can be controlled while others cannot be, except by the use of highly complex and sophisticated equipment not to be found in the average kitchen. It is therefore desirable to control at least what can easily be controlled, for example, accuracy in measuring ingredients.

I prefer to weigh most ingredients used in baking, because the effects of humidity vary less in weight than in measure. Measuring is fine, too, as long as one does not take too casual an approach—such as tapping a measuring cup to level off the flour, or using a liquid measure for dry ingredients, both of which can throw off a recipe substantially.

My idea of heaven includes enough cows and chickens to supply my baking with all the unpasteurized, high-butterfat cream I need for whipping cream and butter and all the wonderfully flavored eggs that chickens which are left to scratch around for their own choice of food can produce. (This fantasy includes training the cows to wait at least until 9 a.m. for milking time.)

Relatively few ingredients are used in baking: most desserts revolve around butter, sugar, flour, eggs, cream, chocolate, nuts, vanilla. Use the best ingredients available—this is as important as technique. For me, texture and flavor come before appearance. I would prefer to have a cake frosted simply and elegantly with buttercream made from butter rather than an exquisitely elaborate design using vegetable-shortening "buttercream."

I find most desserts and cakes made in bakeries both here and abroad are far too sweet for my taste. Sweetness is relatively easy to modify—for chocolate desserts, use bitter-sweet instead of extra-bittersweet if you prefer a sweeter overall taste. A small variation in the amount of sugar will not alter most cake formulas. Meringues, however, need the full amount of sugar used in proportion to the egg white, so, if they are too sweet for your taste, serve them with unsweetened whipped cream and fruit.

Some of the cakes in this book are fairly complicated and time-consuming. I have chosen these recipes for teaching, not only because they are delicious but because they demonstrate several important techniques used in classic baking. Many parts of the recipes can be prepared well in advance—some freeze well, and of course a whole separate dessert can be created often from just one or two components of a more elaborate one.

The formulas for basic Génoise convey an understanding of how Génoise is made and the ratio of different ingredients in relation to each other. Once one understands the how and why it becomes possible to alter things to suit individual taste. One student once confided in another that she was afraid to tell me she made my Grand Marnier cake using a packaged mix and Galliano instead of Grand Marnier for the syrup. I was delighted to hear that she understood the concept of a cake syrup and used it to suit her own purposes and taste. That is the whole point of learning and teaching.

Students often ask me when to serve certain of the more elaborate cakes. Ideally, my preference is to serve them almost as a meal in themselves, such as for a mid-afternoon tea or a late evening after-theater treat. It seems a pity to spend hours producing a subtle, exquisitely delicious dessert only to serve it to guests no longer hungry after a good dinner. But such is the nature of desserts that it is not really unusual to find someone who moments ago was too full for one more mouthful of roast eagerly consuming a piece of cake.

Equipment

In general, I find that equipment designed to stand up to the heavy use imposed by restaurants suits me too. Fortunately, the trend seems to be toward making these commercial products more and more available to the consumer, and special equipment or ingredients listed in this book can be purchased at local gourmet and specialty shops, bakers' supply houses or by mail from my cooking school store: Cordon Rose, 110 Bleecker Street, New York, New York 10012.

OVENS

Five years ago, I chose a Garland commercial range in place of an engagement ring. While I do not entirely regret my choice, I must admit that for baking it is less than ideal. The heat of the enormous oven, great for large roasts, is not very even when it comes to cake making. (It is through this fault that I discovered how beneficial to the production of even cake layers it is to turn pans around halfway through the baking time.) I have also discovered that while a restaurant range is adequate for cooking, someone interested in precision baking will choose a convection-type oven with very little head space. This seems to increase the possibility of even heat. I find that countertop convection ovens, while still not perfectly even, are close to ideal for small cakes. They are also wonderful for puff pastry, *pâte à chou*, meringues and for air-drying buttercream and marzipan decorations. Beware of models that have a fan at the top blowing directly on the cake's surface—this may cause the cake to fall. For baking, I find that setting the temperature at 50 degrees below the temperature specified for conventional ovens works well.

THERMOMETERS

I have never found a thermometer designed for home use that was adequately accurate except for the Taylor instant-reading thermometer, and as this has a small dial, it is not suitable for all purposes. This saddens me in light of the blind faith the consumer seems to place in this one item above all others. So many times absolutely

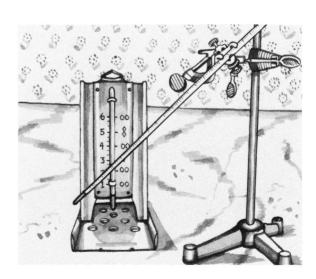

mystified students have reported failure to me, insisting that it couldn't be a problem in temperature because the thermometer said such and such, and a thermometer can't be wrong. Ha!

I finally went to a producer of scientific laboratory thermometers and designed two thermometers, one with a range suitable for work with chocolate and another that is all-purpose and works for chocolate, for sugar syrups and deep-fat frying. For added safety in a class situation I use a laboratory stand and clamp to hold them in place, but as they are all glass, they can safely be held by hand because they do not conduct heat from the liquid in which they are immersed. They can also be used to take the temperature of a refrigerator, freezer or oven, although I do not find them too convenient to read for oven temperature. An excellent commercial oven thermometer available for the consumer is the HB. Even the finest thermometers will have minor deviations, unless of course you purchase one guaranteed by the U.S. Bureau of Standards, which costs more than $100. A conscientious range repairman will come equipped with two thermometers and work from an average taken between the two of them.

SCALE

I prefer to use a commercial-type "portion control" scale such as the Edlund or Pelouze. Portion control enables you to use any bowl to weigh ingredients, because you can place the bowl on top and set the scale to zero, thus taking away the weight of the bowl. As each ingredient is added, it is possible to set the scale back again to zero, which is a great convenience. For greater accuracy in small amounts I prefer a scale whose range does not exceed 5 pounds and with weight divisions of ½ ounce.

MIXER

I have both the K5A (Kitchen Aid) and Kenwood Major, which are heavy-duty, commercial-type mixers. Because I often mix up many large batches of very stiff royal icing, I find it reassuring to know that the Kenwood has a protective device on its motor to keep it from burning out when overheated. I also prefer the shape of its beaters and the tilt-back feature to those of the Kitchen Aid. Both machines, however, are more than adequate for heavy use and because the bowls are conical in shape, it is not necessary to scrape the sides often while mixing.

Any electric mixer with bowl attached will be fine for all the recipes in this book; however, a hand-held mixer is just not powerful enough for the really stiff mixtures such as boiled or royal icing. If your mixer comes equipped with both a flat beater and a balloon whisk, use the flat beater for all-purpose beating and the whisk beater whenever the aim is to beat as much air as possible into the mixture, such as for egg whites, or whole eggs and sugar for Génoise. If your mixer comes with two sizes of bowls, do not use the large one for a small amount of mixture; if only the tips of the beaters come in contact with the mixture, they will not beat effectively.

I find pouring-shields more cumbersome than helpful. When adding ingredients such as flour or confectioners' sugar, which tend to fly about, I drape a large piece of clear plastic wrap over the top of the mixer, including the top of the bowl. Any powdery substance that leaps up does not cling to the plastic as it would to a cloth towel, and the plastic enables you to see what is happening to the mixture.

FLAN RINGS
Flan rings come in many different sizes and shapes; there is even one from France that is adjustable from 7 to 14 inches in diameter. They may be used in place of cake pans in conjunction with a flat baking sheet. If the baking sheet is not absolutely level (or the flan ring is slightly bent), a small amount of batter may leak out around the edges. To prevent this, before placing the flan ring on the sheet, put down three layers of paper towels covered by one layer of parchment. The softness of the towels will allow the flan to sink slightly, closing up any small gaps.

PARCHMENT
This has many uses in baking and decorating. Parchment contains natural oils, and so, unlike waxed paper, does not require greasing when used to line pans. It comes in long rolls, individual sheets, rounds and triangles for parchment decorating cones. I use parchment cones instead of pastry bags when using food coloring that might stain the bags and also when working with a particularly heat-sensitive frosting; the stiffness of the parchment prevents the hand from coming as close to the frosting as with a cloth bag, so the frosting remains firmer for a longer time.

TURNTABLES
An inexpensive Rubbermaid plastic turntable works about as well as a heavyweight, footed, commercial one. Either can be elevated to an ideal work height by being placed on a large, inverted cake pan. (This will help to prevent "decorator's back!")

CARDBOARD ROUNDS
Corrugated cardboard cake rounds are available commercially in many sizes and can also be cut from a box. A doily can be attached to the cardboard using a loop of scotch tape or double-faced tape, or the cake can be placed directly on the cardboard, using a dab of frosting to hold it in place. Cardboard rounds are useful when you are frosting a cake by holding the bottom of the cake in the palm of your hand, and they make the cake easily transportable.

FOLDER/SKIMMER
A medium-sized or large skimmer makes an ideal folder, because the small holes provide just the right resistance to help incorporate flour into a beaten-egg mixture. It helps to bend back the handle slightly.

SERRATED KNIFE
A long-bladed serrated knife is irreplaceable for cutting cakes into layers. If used only for cakes, it will maintain its sharp edge for a lifetime.

Ingredients

BAKER'S JOY

This is an expensive product, but it is the only one which, in my opinion, eliminates the need to line the bottom of a pan with parchment. When I am in a rush, it's great to have around.

BAKING POWDER

Baking powder must be stored in an airtight container because humidity will deactivate some of its power. There is also a substantial loss of strength in baking powder that is more than a year old. Date the bottom of the can when you first buy it, or write the expiration date on the lid. To check if it is still active, drop a spoonful in hot water. The directions on the can say that it should bubble enthusiastically, but as people's conceptions of enthusiasm may vary, it is preferable to depend on the dating system.

BAKING SODA

Baking soda has three important purposes in my baking life: it is great for putting out kitchen fires (though a fire in a saucepan needs only a lid to extinguish it by depriving it of oxygen—I remember a class I taught on the Gâteau au Grand Marnier when the Grand Marnier glaze caught fire and even though a student came rushing at me with a lid, I yelled before I could stop myself: "*Not* the baking soda!"); to neutralize some of the acid in a cake baked with choco-late or sour cream; and to peel the ever-recalcitrant hazelnut. The peel on a hazelnut is particularly bitter and also particularly difficult to remove using any other system. (Thank you, Carl Sontheimer—for this I will always be grateful!)

To peel hazelnuts (filberts), place a half cup of nuts (2½ ounces) in a saucepan containing 1½ cups of boiling water. Add 2 tablespoons of baking soda, and boil 3 minutes. Test a nut by running it under cold water to see if the peel slips off easily. If not, boil a few minutes longer. Rinse the nuts well under cold running water and crisp or brown them in a 350-degree oven (20 minutes to brown). (Note: the baking soda turns the peel almost black.) Peaches may be peeled with the same effect—minus the crisping, of course.

Baking soda is responsible for the reddish cast to a chocolate cake. Although it improves the cake's flavor, it also contributes a slight coarseness in texture.

FINE DRY BREADCRUMBS

These are used to line the pan for very delicate mixtures such as the Chocolate Cloud Roll. They do not get absorbed into the cake itself—they merely enable the cake to be released from the parchment. If you buy commercial breadcrumbs (unseasoned, of course), you may have to pulverize them slightly in the food processor if they are too coarse, but do not allow them to become too powdery. To make your own, place slices of crustless bread in the oven with only the pilot light on and leave overnight or until they dry out. If your oven does not have a pilot light, dry bread at about 200 degrees for a few hours. Store the crumbs tightly covered in the refrigerator and they will keep almost indefinitely. (Zwieback makes wonderful flavorless breadcrumbs that never become rancid.)

BUTTER

All the butter used in these recipes is unsalted. Sweet, unsalted butter has a better flavor. If you can find only lightly salted butter in your market, there are three choices: make your own butter (recipe follows), remove the salt from the butter, or omit salt from the recipe. To remove salt, place the butter in large bowl filled with water and ice cubes and knead it for several minutes. Dry it thoroughly using paper towels. European butter has an 84 percent butterfat content, American has 80 percent. Less expensive brands

generally use 10 percent whey cream, which is a by-product of cheese production.

Butter graded *A* or *AA* has a lower water content and is more desirable than others. If the butter remains fairly soft even after refrigeration, and if, when you cut the butter, small droplets of water appear, the water content is relatively high. Excess water can be removed from butter using the same method as for the removal of salt.

To make your own butter, place heavy cream in a food processor and process it until it begins to thicken. For every cup of cream add two tablespoons of cold water. Process it until the cream separates. Strain out the liquid (this ''buttermilk'' is unsoured and delicious to drink), and dry the resulting butter thoroughly with paper towels. One cup of cream yields about three ounces of butter. Unlike commercial butter, this butter keeps only about a week in the refrigerator. (Commercial butter is made from cream with a higher butterfat content and is churned immediately after flash pasteurization.)

For clarified butter, see Génoise on page 31.

When buying commercial butter, the way to decide which brand has the best flavor—and flavor does vary significantly—is to hold a blind tasting. Have someone offer you three or four samples of butter without knowing which brand is which until after you decide on your preference.

Butter freezes very well with little loss of flavor for up to two years. Be sure to allow it to defrost before using it to clarify or sauté, because frozen butter melted over heat burns instead of browning. To store, wrap it well, as butter absorbs other odors very readily. Do not wrap it directly in foil, because the butter may pick up its metal odor.

CHOCOLATE

People who love chocolate seem to love it with an almost addictive passion. It has been speculated that the presence of phenylethylamine (a natural chemical produced by the brain itself), found in chocolate in minute quantities, may act as a mild stimulant and mood elevator and is perhaps indirectly responsible for the association of delicious taste with pleasant feeling. It is considered to be responsible for causing headaches in those few unfortunate people who have an allergic reaction to it.

Chocolate is one of the major ingredients in my cakes and buttercreams. Working with it as much as I do, I have found there is an enormous difference in both texture and flavor between different brands. The best way to determine your own favorite is by blind-taste tests. I prefer to use the finest quality chocolate in my desserts. My own favorite is Lindt or Tobler extra-bittersweet. Recently, Lindt has stopped exporting this particular variety to the United States.

When my distributor first discovered that I was using Lindt and Tobler chocolate bars for baking, he said in a shocked voice: "But it's *eating* chocolate!" Somehow it didn't seem to occur to him that baked and frozen desserts are eaten as well. It may seem like an obvious discovery in retrospect, but it took me years to discover that the major reason certain famous bakeries and restaurants are able to produce such delicious chocolate desserts is because of the quality of chocolate they use. So taste the chocolate before you bake with it—if you don't like the taste and texture now, you probably won't like it any better in the completed dessert.

In the less expensive chocolates, I find that Nestlé's semi-sweet morsels have an excellent flavor, although they lack the smoothness of the Swiss chocolate.

Different brands of chocolate differ partly because of special formulas unique to each company, which determine the blend of the beans, the type and amount of flavorings and the proportion of chocolate liquor and cocoa butter.

Taste and texture are also greatly affected by the length of roasting, grinding and conching. Grinding reduces particle size, and conching—a wavelike motion—releases volatile oils, develops flavor and coats the sugar particles with cocoa butter, which reduces the feeling of gritty abrasiveness. Too much conching can result in an oily texture. European, particularly Swiss, chocolate is usually conched for up to 96 hours, which produces the velvety-smooth texture Europeans favor and Americans generally consider to be too rich. American chocolate may be conched for only 4 to 5 hours, or not at all, although there are some brands that claim 74 hours of conching.

Lecithin is an emulsifier found in soya beans which is used to stabilize chocolate. Its presence reduces the amount of cocoa butter required to cover the surface area of particles. It frees the cocoa butter to act as a floating medium for the particles. It also reduces viscosity, although the addition of too much lecithin will do the reverse, due to its own viscosity. This is only one illustration of the complexity involved in the production of fine chocolate.

The U.S. government provides certain restrictions or classifications for chocolate that dictate the type of fat and percentage of chocolate liquor. To be classified as real chocolate, it must contain no fat other than cocoa butter.

Pure Chocolate

Pure chocolate, otherwise known as bitter, baking or unsweetened chocolate, contains only chocolate liquor (cocoa solids and cocoa butter) and flavorings. Depending on the variety of the bean used, 50 to 58 percent of the chocolate liquor is cocoa butter. (This is the same amount present in the nibs—the term for the cocoa bean after removal of the pod—before processing.) No lecithin may be added, but a great variety of flavorings are permissible, such as vanilla or

vanillin, ground nuts, coffee, salt and various extracts.

Cocoa
Cocoa is the pure chocolate liquor with about three-quarters of the cocoa butter removed. The remaining cocoa is then pulverized. Dutch process means that the cocoa has been treated with a mild alkalin to mellow the flavor and make it more soluble.

Bitter-Sweet or Semi-Sweet
Bitter-sweet or semi-sweet and extra-bitter-sweet (for which there is no U.S. government standard) is the pure chocolate liquor with sugar, vanilla or vanillin and extra cocoa butter added. Semi-sweet morsels have to be more viscous to maintain their chip shape during baking. *Couverture* for use in candy dipping usually refers to compound chocolate in the United States. There is no standard for the European *couverture*, which is produced with a high percentage of cocoa butter, resulting in low viscosity and subsequently a thin and glossy coating when used in candy dipping.

Milk Chocolate
Milk chocolate contains the pure chocolate liquor, milk solids, butter, vanilla or vanillin and extra cocoa butter.

White Chocolate
White chocolate is not considered to be "real chocolate" in the United States because it contains no cocoa solids. The better qualities are, however, made with cocoa butter, and have a delicious flavor. White chocolate also contains lecithin, milk solids and vanilla or vanillin. When melted, it hardens faster than dark chocolate but is softer at room temperature. Its shelf life is slightly shorter than that of regular chocolate.

Compound Chocolate
Compound chocolate is classified as chocolate "flavor," because instead of cocoa butter it contains vegetable shortening such as soya, palm kernel or coconut oil. This type of fat is more stable than cocoa butter and also affords the chocolate a higher melting point, which means it can be heated to a higher temperature. For this reason it is sometimes referred to as "summer coating." Its taste is acceptable, some people find it delicious (they can't have tasted Lindt or Tobler), but it lacks the complexity and fullness of a fine-quality chocolate. Still, for small, decorative touches when one doesn't have time to temper chocolate, it is a joy to have on hand.

The following table lists the average amount of chocolate liquor and the total amount of cocoa butter contained in different types of chocolate.

Note that because chocolate liquor is composed of cocoa solids and cocoa butter, the amount of cocoa butter listed includes that cocoa butter *plus* any additional quantity necessary to make up the total. Where there is a U.S. government standard listed, this requires only a minimum amount of chocolate liquor; it does not control cocoa butter as such. U.S. standards for chocolate content apply worldwide.

Cocoa (breakfast cocoa): at least 22 to 25 percent cocoa butter

Cocoa (regular): 10 to 21 percent cocoa butter

Bitter or unsweetened baking chocolate: pure chocolate liquor, 50 to 58 percent cocoa butter, averaging 53 percent

Couverture chocolate: 40 to 51 percent chocolate liquor, at least 34 percent cocoa butter (no U.S. standard)

Extra-bitter-sweet chocolate: 50 percent chocolate liquor, 30 percent cocoa butter (no U.S. standard)

Semi-sweet or bitter-sweet chocolate: 35 percent chocolate liquor, 27 percent cocoa butter (U.S. standard)

Semi-sweet bits: 29 percent chocolate liquor, about 29 percent cocoa butter (no U.S. standard)

Sweet chocolate: 15 percent chocolate liquor, 27 percent cocoa butter (U.S. standard)

Milk chocolate: 10 percent chocolate liquor; minimum of 12 percent whole milk; 29 to 33 percent cocoa butter (U.S. standard)

Storing Chocolate

The best way to store chocolate or cocoa is to keep it well wrapped in an airtight container (chocolate is quick to absorb other odors and must not be exposed to dampness), and at a temperature of 60 to 75 degrees with less than 50 percent relative humidity. Under these conditions, chocolate should keep well for at least two years. I have heard that chocolate stored at ideal conditions can keep for years and will even age like a fine wine.

Melting Chocolate

The greatest enemy of chocolate is water. One droplet of water or steam is enough to cause chocolate to "tighten" (thicken undesirably), and can ruin an entire batch. It is possible to melt chocolate in water for certain purposes as long as there is at least one tablespoon per ounce of chocolate. When a mixture of chocolate and water is heated, the particles of chocolate expand, causing the mixture to thicken much in the same way that cornstarch behaves. (During the roasting of the nibs, the particles dry, thus producing their ability to absorb moisture in this way.)

If tightening does occur, it is possible to restore the chocolate to a workable condition by the addition of either vegetable shortening, cocoa butter or clarified butter. Nothing, however, will restore chocolate that has been scorched from overheating. The ideal way to melt chocolate gently is in the oven with only the heat of a pilot light. This takes at least half an hour, but chocolate can even be left in the oven overnight. *Never* cover melting chocolate, because moisture formed on the lid may drop onto the chocolate, causing it to tighten. If you are using a double boiler, make sure the water does not touch the bottom of the upper container, or the chocolate will overheat. Be sure, also, that the water is not simmering, which would produce steam.

Tempering Chocolate

The ideal situation for working with chocolate is a cool, dry, draft-free area, 65 to 70 degrees Fahrenheit. At 74 degrees the chocolate is still workable, but if it gets much hotter, you may encounter problems.

Remember that direct sunlight produces in-

tense heat (solar energy). I will always remember the night I left an assortment of perfectly tempered, heart-shaped chocolate praline cutouts on my marble worktop as a special treat for next day's class. We found a melted pool of chocolate praline the next morning. The early morning sun's rays had found their way unerringly to the chocolate. You have to think of everything!

Chocolate, when used for candy making or decorative work, has a reputation for being extremely temperamental. To insure consistency of results—chocolate that sets quickly and firmly with a high gloss and no gray streaks or spots known as "bloom" (a pretty word to describe a dreaded condition)—it is necessary either to use compound chocolate or to temper the chocolate.

Bloom will occur in any chocolate (even compound chocolate) subjected to a sudden and extreme change in temperature. It disappears on melting.

There is no need to temper white chocolate—because of its color the bloom would not be apparent—except to insure ease in unmolding. For coating, white chocolate is brought to a slightly higher temperature than regular chocolate (92 degrees), because it forms too thick a coat at lower temperatures.

Professional candy makers use a "*couverture chocolate*" that has more cocoa butter and lower viscosity. This is ideal for coating candies because it makes it possible to achieve a thin coating with a high gloss. A small amount of cocoa butter, vegetable or mineral oil may be added to other types of chocolate if a thinner coat is desired.

Cocoa butter is a complex mixture of fats, each having a different melting and setting point. Tempering is accomplished by bringing the chocolate to a temperature of 110 to 115 degrees, a point at which all fat is melted and equally distributed; then spreading it on a smooth surface to assist in rapid cooling, during which some of the fat fractions set (at about 80 to 82 degrees); then slightly reheating it (depending on the type of chocolate) to a specific temperature so that the fat fractions remain crystallized to act as nuclei on which complete crystallization will occur when the chocolate finally sets. Cocoa butter will form crystal structures at four to five possible different temperatures. In tempering, one is attempting to secure the most stable of the crystal structures to produce a chocolate that is less likely to "melt in your hand."

If chocolate is allowed to exceed 120 degrees, there will be a loss of flavor and gloss. If, during reheating, the ideal temperature is exceeded, some of the fat fractions may melt, causing cocoa particles to drop, leaving spots of cocoa butter or bloom, and the resulting chocolate will not set quickly or unmold effectively. Milk chocolate, for example, contains butter, which has a lower melting point than cocoa butter, so its ideal dipping temperature must be lower than for semi-sweet chocolate. The ideal temperature range is when the chocolate is thick enough to set quickly and thin enough to coat adequately but not excessively. If the temperature is too low, the coating will be thick and dull; if too high, then the chocolate must be cooled down to

80 to 82 degrees and reheated to the proper temperature. These are the ultrarefined, painstaking methods used by the *confiseur* or candy maker. For less delicate and demanding chocolate work, such as shavings or cutouts, there are three easier methods.

Heating the Chocolate (for all methods)

It is important not to melt chocolate over direct heat because you risk overheating. However, I have recently discovered that the new Salton hot-tray models have a temperature control that is capable of maintaining unusually low temperatures—below 110 degrees. This means that for the initial heating, I can leave the chocolate in the pan on the hot tray for several hours until I am ready to use it. Then it is only a matter of moments to bring the chocolate to the precise temperature for tempering. After cooling, I again return the pan directly to the hot tray and, watching carefully, bring it up to the correct working temperature. To check the heat of your hot tray, place water and a thermometer in a saucepan so that the thermometer is well immersed for an accurate reading. Set the control to the lowest number possible and take a temperature reading over a period of about 2 hours, adjusting the control as necessary until you are certain that the heat will never exceed 110 degrees.

If you are using a double boiler, make sure that the upper container does not touch the water and that the water does not exceed 140 degrees. Remember that the residual heat of the container can bring the temperature of the chocolate to as much as 5 degrees higher than it registered when it was removed from the heat, so never allow the thermometer to exceed 110 degrees. Also remember to wipe all moisture from the bottom of the container so that it doesn't drip on the chocolate when you pour it. While tempering the chocolate, stir it continuously to blend the cocoa butter and, if you are using a double boiler, it is important to stir it to prevent parts of the chocolate from melting unevenly and overheating. Stir slowly so as not to

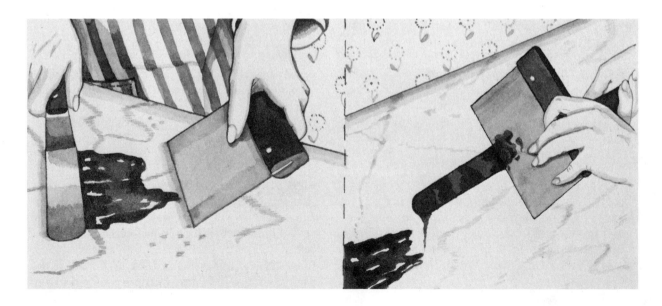

create air bubbles, which require much tapping of the pan on the counter to eliminate!

METHOD ONE:

This is the most precise and painstaking method, and will result in the thinnest, most glossy coat, and predictable set. It is the most appropriate method for dipping.

Chop or grate the chocolate and bring it to 110 to 115 degrees. Remove it from the heat and stir it a few seconds to cool. Pour about two-thirds of the melted chocolate onto a smooth, cool surface such as marble or formica (leaving the rest in a container), and spread it, preferably using an angled metal spatula and a plastic scraper. Scrape the chocolate toward the center, clean the scraper with the spatula and spread it again, continuing this process until the chocolate just begins to set (it will be about 80 to 82 degrees). Scrape it immediately into the container (do not allow the chocolate to harden), and return it to the heat, stirring continuously. It will require very little heat to reach the proper working temperature.

METHOD TWO:

This is a faster method, suitable for most decorative purposes such as cutouts, cigars and leaves. It is also fine for truffles that are going to be dusted with cocoa. The gradual addition of grated chocolate to the already melted chocolate helps to cool it to the proper working temperature and acts as a catalyst in forming the emulsion with the cocoa butter.

Chop or grate the chocolate, reserving about one-third. Bring the larger amount of chocolate to 110 to 115 degrees and remove it from the heat. Add the reserved chocolate 1 tablespoon at a time, stirring until it is cooled to the proper temperature.

METHOD THREE:

This is the same as Method Two, except that instead of adding finely grated chocolate, stir in one large piece of chocolate and remove it when the correct temperature has been reached. Wrap the lump in plastic wrap until it sets and use it again at another melting.

METHOD FOUR:

The addition of extra cocoa butter, clarified butter, vegetable shortening or oil helps to keep the existing cocoa butter in suspension, enables the chocolate to set faster and results in added gloss. It also thins out the chocolate enough to produce a less heavy coating. For dark chocolate use 1 tablespoon of oil for 3 ounces of chocolate. Milk chocolate and white chocolate are softer, so use only 1 teaspoon of oil for 3 ounces of chocolate. Chop or grate the chocolate and stir it together with the oil. Heat until melted and cool to working temperature.

Dipping, Molding and Spreading Temperatures for Chocolate

If you are depending on a thermometer, be sure it is an accurate one. The thermometer that I designed (see *Equipment*, Thermometers) is easy to read and accurate to within a fraction of a degree. It should be immersed 1 inch for a truly accurate reading. An oral thermometer from a drug store is harder to read but a lot more accurate than the average candy thermometer.

Temperatures for Dipping, Molding or Spreading

Compound chocolate (summer coating):	100 degrees
White chocolate:	92 degrees
Dark chocolate:	88-91 degrees
Milk chocolate:	84-87 degrees

If you are not using a thermometer when cooling chocolate to final working temperatures (used in some of the above methods), dab a spot of chocolate just under your lower lip. The temperature will be correct when it just begins to feel cool. For compound chocolate, which should be just above body temperature, chocolate should feel just barely warm. Of course, if you have a beard, as my husband points out, you really would be better off investing in a good thermometer!

COCOA BUTTER
When substituting one type of chocolate for another it sometimes becomes necessary to add shortening. The ideal shortening to add is cocoa butter, because it is a natural component of chocolate. Clarified butter (all water is removed) also works well and contributes a better flavor than vegetable shortening. Pure cocoa butter is available in some pharmacies. Kept refrigerated, it will stay fresh for several years.

CORN SYRUP AND GLUCOSE
Corn syrup is an invert sugar, identical to glucose except that it has a higher water content. To convert corn syrup to glucose, bring 1 cup of light corn syrup to a full boil and remove it from the heat. Allow it to cool completely and stir in an additional ½ cup of corn syrup. This will approximate the texture of glucose. Corn syrup has approximately half the sweetening power of sugar. Glucose, which is more concentrated, has slightly more sweetening power than corn syrup.

CORNSTARCH
Cornstarch has half the thickening power of flour and produces a clearer, more translucent sauce or glaze. It thickens by absorbing liquid and expanding, and this absorption can take place only when the liquid has reached a full boil. It is very important not to stir vigorously after thickening has occurred, because this will break down the cell structure of the cornstarch, release the liquid, and the mixture will become watery.

Cornstarch is smooth and silky, and is sometimes used in small proportions to replace part of the cake flour, as for Génoise. This produces a cake with a tighter grain and one that is there-

fore somewhat moister. Potato starch may be substituted in equal proportion for the cornstarch, but will result in a slightly drier, less soft crumb.

CREAM
Having instructed you how to make your own butter from cream I shall now tell you how to reverse the process to make a better cream from butter. Why make your own cream? Because cream with a higher butterfat content is more stable and does not water-out when making whipped cream; also because in some areas it is virtually impossible to find anything but that dreadful ultrapasteurized version that is both more difficult to whip and lacks flavor.

There are two home cream makers on the market to date—both from England—one manual (the Bel Cream Maker) and the other an attachment to the Kenwood electric mixer. The two operate on the same principle: milk and butter are heated together until the butter is melted. The mixture is pumped through a small pin-sized opening, the pressure of which rehomogenizes it into what it once was: cream.

The butterfat content obviously depends on the ratio of butter to milk. To make extra-heavy cream, ideal for whipping and usually available only in bakery wholesale outlets, use equal weights of butter and milk.

If only salted butter is available, desalt it in the following way: For every 4 ounces (8 tablespoons) of butter, use 2 cups of water. Boil the butter in water for 2 to 3 minutes. Allow it to cool until the butter solidifies and forms a crust on top of the water. Remove the butter and heat it with the milk as for unsalted butter.

According to law, heavy cream must contain between 20 and 40 percent butterfat. Most brands have about 37.5 percent. The percentage is not required to be listed on the container; however, in comparing brands, I have noticed that when I shake a container, the cream with the higher butterfat sloshes around the container in a heavier way. Half-and-half contains 12 percent butterfat. Light cream contains 18 percent.

The stability of whipped cream is also increased significantly both by an acid medium and by a cold temperature while beating. This is especially important to remember when dealing with ultrapasteurized cream, but also keeps all heavy cream from watering-out, especially in warm, humid weather. Cream may be beaten over a bowl of iced water or the bowl and the beater can be well chilled before use. A copper beating bowl (normally used for egg whites) or a few drops of lemon juice or yogurt do well to produce the acid medium, if all else fails.

I usually place cream, confectioners' sugar and vanilla in a mixing bowl with a beater and refrigerate the mixture until it is very cold. I beat it with the electric mixer only until I can see the marks in the cream, and then I finish the beating with a whisk. For frosting and piping I usually further stabilize the whipped cream with a tiny bit of gelatin or corn syrup, and beat it just until stiff peaks form. For all other purposes I beat the cream only until it mounds softly when dropped from a spoon. It is delicious this way, and even when spread in a cake roll, the texture becomes firmer with time and is more pleasant than a stiffer whipped cream.

To hold whipped cream from anywhere between 1 hour and 1 day, line a strainer with cheesecloth and suspend it over a bowl. Place the whipped cream in the strainer and cover it with plastic wrap or foil, as cream (like butter) is quick to absorb any odors in the refrigerator. A cup of cream, whipped, can lose up to 2 tablespoons of liquid. When you are ready to use the cream, discard the liquid, place the cream in a bowl and stir it very lightly. A teaspoon or two of corn syrup beaten into the cream helps to keep it from watering-out.

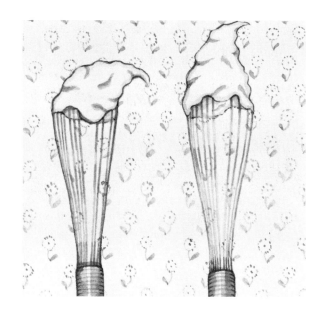

One cup of cream when whipped will approximately double in volume; whipping by hand, with a wire balloon whisk results in the best volume and stability. Fresh cream will not whip. It must be aged for at least 2 days.

EGGS

All these recipes use USDA grade large eggs. If you find it more economical to use extra-large or jumbo eggs, be sure to measure them in a liquid measure and convert the amount (see Weights of Ingredients chart, next section). When using 4 eggs in a recipe, the difference between large and jumbo can mean that you've added a whole extra egg and this is significant to the results of the recipe. Both yolks and whites freeze well but yolks require the addition of about half a teaspoon of sugar per yolk. Remember to subtract this amount of sugar from the recipe.

Beating Egg Whites

Eggs achieve their greatest volume when they are at room temperature when beaten. They are easier to separate when cold; however, the yolks may develop a dry film, which has to be discarded. To avoid this film it is possible to brush the yolks with a thin film of oil or spray them lightly with Pam without altering their texture or flavor. To warm eggs quickly to room temperature, place them (still in the shell) in very warm water for 5 minutes.

Very fresh egg whites (under 2 days old) give poor volume when beaten. In general, the more viscous (thicker) the white, the less volume will result. To age the whites you may freeze them overnight, and when you thaw them the next day they will have broken down sufficiently. It is also possible to beat them only enough to break down the viscosity and allow them to sit overnight at room temperature. A pinch of salt (⅛ teaspoon for 2 whites) also serves to break down the protein and loosen up the white. If whites are to be used in a dessert that will not in any way be cooked—a mousse, for example—it is preferable to sacrifice a little of the volume and use eggs that are not too old, because their flavor is better.

Whole eggs when beaten at room temperature increase from four to six times in volume, egg whites seven times. Grease will keep the whites from beating into a stiff mass. Be sure no egg yolk falls into the whites and that the bowl and beater are very clean. When using a copper beating bowl, wash it with salt and vinegar and rinse it well before each use.

Sugar, when added to egg white, results in slightly less volume but a great increase in stability. For example, it is virtually impossible to overbeat a meringue, because of its high proportion of sugar to egg white. Whenever you see a recipe that calls for all the sugar to be beaten with the yolks, remove a couple of tablespoons to be beaten with the whites. Whites with more stability lose less volume when being incorporated into other mixtures. When adding sugar, pour it onto the sides of the mixing bowl and not directly onto the egg-white mass—this will prevent it from deflating the whites. Confectioners' sugar contains cornstarch, which deflates whites, so when this is used—as for meringues—it is usually folded in at the end.

A copper beating bowl provides the ideal acid medium for stabilizing egg whites without imparting any discernible flavor. This enables the whites to be beaten to a greater volume without danger of their separating. This is not a myth: I have performed extensive tests under identical conditions.

A few drops of lemon juice will help increase stability, and cream of tartar (⅛ teaspoon per white, increased to 3/16 teaspoon on a very humid day) is also extremely effective in stabilizing egg whites with a very slight loss of volume. The latter, however, imparts a definite zing, experienced on the tip of the tongue, which dissipates during baking but may linger on if the whites are to be used uncooked.

The ideal way to beat whites for maximum volume and stability is: Add salt and start beating slowly until frothy; add cream of tartar to the mixture; add 1 tablespoon of the sugar and raise the beater to high. When very soft peaks form, gradually add the remaining sugar. Beat until the peaks become stiff but no further, or the white will be difficult to incorporate into mixtures. As you will notice, the beater speed is on an upward progression. Once raised, it must never be lowered, though it may be stopped momentarily to check the stiffness of the whites.

FLOUR
Although I have given you the approximate equivalents to use if you substitute all-purpose flour for cake flour (see next section), I must in all honesty report that the results will differ. All-purpose flour is made of a blend of hard summer

and soft winter wheats. Hard wheat contains more protein, providing a great deal of gluten which, when activated, contributes structure. While this is wonderful for puff pastry, overmixing a cake batter can result in a coarse, tough texture. Soft wheat is high in starch and absorbs fat and moisture more quickly. If you feel the two flours by rubbing them between your fingertips, you will notice how much smoother and silkier the cake flour feels. This helps to result in cakes with a softer, more velvety crumb. Unbleached flour contains more gluten than bleached because some of it is destroyed during the bleaching process.

When recipes tell you to sift together dry ingredients, this is not sufficient to blend them evenly. Sifting actually accomplishes something more important: by aerating the dry ingredients, it helps them to mix more readily with the moist ingredients. To blend dry ingredients whisk or stir them together or place them in the mixing bowl of an electric mixer and beat them for a minute or so.

I measure flour either by sifting it directly into the cup and leveling it off with a metal spatula or knife, or by the "dip-and-sweep" system of dipping the measuring cup into the flour until the flour is heaped on top and then, using a metal spatula or blade, sweeping off the excess. "One cup of flour, sifted," means that first you measure the flour, then sift it. "One cup of sifted flour" means you measure by sifting it into the cup. I use different systems in different recipes simply because the different amounts of flour needed are sometimes easier to measure one way, sometimes the other. Never tap a measuring cup to level flour, it will settle the flour in the cup and you will wind up with much more flour than was intended.

Do not store flour near heat as it will dry out. (It contains a certain amount of natural moisture.)

GELATIN
When a recipe calls for 1 package of gelatin, use 1 package. When it requires half a package take care, because the package states that it contains 1 tablespoon of gelatin (3 teaspoons) and it actually contains 2 teaspoons, so half a package means 1 teaspoon!

GLYCERINE
Glycerine is a clear, tasteless liquid made from fats and oils. In a rolled fondant it contributes softness, smoothness and sheen. It is ideal for thinning paste food colors and thickening melted chocolate for writing.

NUTS
Nuts will keep for well over a year in the freezer. They may be used without defrosting, but if you plan to grind them it is better to defrost them first. A tablespoon or so of cornstarch or flour borrowed from the rest of the recipe will help to keep them from becoming greasy. This will not be a problem if you are using a rotary grater or food processor equipped with a pulse. (For easy peeling, see Baking Soda.)

PAM
I prefer Pam to the other nonstick vegetable-spray products because it has virtually no odor. It is composed of lecithin—a natural emulsifying agent, a small amount of soybean oil, a minute amount of alcohol and a propellant which dissipates on spraying. Lecithin is often added to chocolate as an emulsifying agent to prevent the grayish bloom caused by the separation of the cocoa butter.

In an emergency, I have sprayed Pam on chocolate decorations to eliminate the bloom caused by too rapid a change from cold to heat. A light spray gave the chocolate a beautiful gleam and covered the gray. (To achieve an even coat, it must sit for 24 hours.) I have even sprayed Pam on my fingers when working with sticky substances. Its uses are endless.

PRALINE PASTE

The best praline paste is made with hazelnuts (filberts), and is extremely difficult to make yourself. I have succeeded with the use of a food processor and the addition of hazelnut oil, but the effort was not worth the expense. Praline paste keeps frozen indefinitely and for at least six months in the refrigerator. It is available at some specialty stores; my store also carries an excellent brand available to commercial bakers.

SUGAR

Superfine sugar dissolves more easily than granulated, and in baking often results in a finer, smoother texture. To make your own, simply place granulated sugar in a food processor or blender and process it until fine. It is impossible to make it too fine—confectioners' sugar, which is merely powdered granulated sugar, requires stone wheels to reduce it to that soft a substance!

Sugar Solutions

Bringing sugar to the various stages and consistencies known as soft ball, firm ball, hard ball, soft crack and hard crack involves making a supersaturated solution from a saturated solution.

A saturated sugar solution contains the maximum amount of sugar possible without it precipitating-out into crystals. By heating the solution, more sugar can dissolve in the same amount of water.

A supersaturated solution is very unstable, and recrystallization can occur from agitation or even just by letting it stand, unless proper heating has taken place.

To make sugar solutions, start with sugar and one-quarter its volume of water. Heat the solution to boiling point, stirring continuously. At this point you may wash down any crystals that have formed on the sides of the pan with a wet pastry brush. (I omit this step and have never had any problems.) From this point on, the solution should never be stirred, as any interference may cause recrystallization.

There are times when it will be necessary to agitate the solution—for example, when dipping cream puffs into caramel, or when repeatedly dipping in a device to make spun sugar. When the solution is destined to be used in this way, it should be prepared with the addition of an "interfering agent" such as cream of tartar, lemon juice, corn syrup or butter, all of which inhibit recrystallization.

The different stages of sugar solutions are measured either by temperature (using a thermometer) or by dropping a small amount into ice water to test the consistency. (Be sure not to dip the same spoon back into the solution until it is cleaned.)

Caramel is extremely difficult to make in humid weather. The caramel just will not harden properly and remains sticky. I was once making several batches of caramel and discovered that by boiling so many sugar solutions I was creating my own humidity and defeating my purpose.

VANILLA

I use only pure vanilla extract except when making a pure white frosting for a wedding cake, when I am forced to use clear vanilla, which is a flavoring and not the pure stuff. I have recently discovered a source for pure vanilla concentrate. It is produced in Grasse, France, home of the perfume manufacturers, and is almost as expensive as perfume, but a few drops go a long way and provide an indescribable aroma. One student placed a drop on her right wrist and a drop of "Joy" perfume on her left and her husband preferred the vanilla! A small plastic squeeze bottle with a pointed tip is an ideal dispenser.

Vanilla beans vary enormously in quality; the best come from Madagascar, Mexico and Tahiti and are about twice the size of and more highly perfumed than the other beans. Place a whole vanilla bean in a bottle of good quality Cognac to be used only for dessert making—it's wonderful in chocolate mousses and chocolate frostings. (It's also good to drink, and can turn an ordinary cup of coffee into something exquisite.)

YEAST

I prefer using fresh yeast when I can get it from a source that guarantees freshness. Fresh yeast seems to work somewhat faster than dried yeast. I'm not sure if there is any difference in flavor, but I feel better about using it. If the fresh yeast isn't absolutely fresh, the final baked product will have a slightly sour taste. Fresh yeast freezes indefinitely, but certain precautions have to be taken in defrosting it. Yeast is a live organism and must be "awakened" gradually from the frozen state. To defrost it, place it in the refrigerator for a minimum of 48 hours. Since a few yeast cells will have been destroyed in the process, use the original amount plus an extra one-quarter.

Measures, Substitutions and Equivalencies, Weights and Volume

All dry ingredients are measured in dry measures by dipping the cup into the bin and sweeping or leveling off the excess with a straight-edge. (This is known as the dip-and-sweep method.)

Liquid ingredients (this includes corn syrup and glucose) are always measured in liquid measures by reading markings at eye level from below the meniscus (the curved upper surface of the liquid). When measuring or weighing small amounts of ingredients, round them off to the nearest convenient measure.

MEASURES:

1½ teaspoons = ½ tablespoon
3 teaspoons = 1 tablespoon
4 tablespoons = ¼ cup
5 tablespoons +1 teaspoon = ⅓ cup
8 tablespoons = ½ cup
10 tablespoons +2 teaspoons = ⅔ cup
12 tablespoons = ¾ cup
16 tablespoons = 1 cup

1 cup = 8 ounces = ½ pint
1 pint = 16 ounces
2 pints = 1 quart = 32 ounces
4 quarts = 1 gallon

1 pound = 16 ounces
¾ pound = 12 ounces
½ pound = 8 ounces
¼ pound = 4 ounces

SUBSTITUTIONS AND APPROXIMATE EQUIVALENCIES:

1 ounce chocolate (semi-sweet) = 3 tablespoons cocoa + 1 tablespoon cocoa butter or shortening

6 ounces semi-sweet chocolate = 2 ounces unsweetened chocolate + 7 tablespoons sugar + 2 tablespoons cocoa butter or shortening

4 ounces extra-bitter-sweet chocolate = about 3 ounces semi-sweet + 1 ounce unsweetened (you will have slightly more cocoa butter and slightly less chocolate liquor)

1 cup self-rising cake flour = 1 cup cake flour + 1½ teaspoons baking powder + ¼-½ teaspoon salt (for a chocolate cake add ¼ teaspoon baking soda per cup of flour)

1 cup sifted cake flour = about 1 cup − 2½ tablespoons unsifted all-purpose flour*

1 cup unsifted cake flour = 1 cup − 2 tablespoons unsifted all-purpose flour*

1 teaspoon baking powder = ⅓ teaspoon baking soda + ½ teaspoon cream of tartar, or ¼ teaspoon baking soda + ½ cup buttermilk (you will need to replace ½ cup of the liquid called for in the recipe with ½ cup buttermilk)

¼-ounce package dry yeast (2½ teaspoons) = ¾ ounce (2 packed teaspoons) compressed or cake yeast

1 cup granulated sugar = 1 cup superfine sugar − 2 teaspoons

*To lower gluten to approximate cake flour, substitute 2 tablespoons cornstarch for 2 tablespoons of the remaining all-purpose flour.

WEIGHTS AND VOLUME:

FLOUR: sifted, all-purpose   1 cup = 4.1 ounces
        unsifted, all-purpose   1 cup = 4.4 ounces
        sifted, cake flour   1 cup = 3.4 ounces
        unsifted, cake flour   1 cup = 3.9 ounces

SUGAR: granulated   1 cup = 6.82 ounces
        superfine*   1 cup = 7.06 ounces
        sifted confectioners'   1 cup = 3.4 ounces
        unsifted confectioners'   1 cup = 4.3 ounces

COCOA: unsifted   1 tablespoon = $\frac{1}{5}$ ounce
                                     1 cup = 3.1 ounces

CHOCOLATE: melted   3 ounces = ¼ cup

BUTTER: 1 cup = 8 ounces
                                     1 tablespoon = ½ ounce

EGGS: USDA graded large   1 egg (in shell) = 2 ounces
                                     1 whole egg = 3 tablespoons +
                                       ⅓ teaspoon
                                     1 yolk = 3⅓ teaspoons
                                     1 white = 2 tablespoons

                                     1 cup whole eggs = about 5 eggs =
                                       8.8 ounces
                                     1 cup yolks = about 14 yolks = 8.2 ounces
                                     1 cup whites = about 8 whites =
                                       8.7 ounces
                                     2 yolks may be substituted for 1 egg

*These weights are for when you are using the "dip and sweep" method. Using "dump" method—spooning into measure as opposed to dipping—superfine sugar weighs slightly less than granulated. This is because it becomes slightly aerated when "dumped."

Recipes

Génoise

Classic Génoise is made from the purest, most straightforward ingredients—flour, eggs, sugar, unsalted butter and vanilla—that are combined to produce a cake of exceptional lightness without reliance upon chemical leavening agents such as baking soda or baking powder. The sponge layers evenly absorb liqueur-based syrups, which both flavor and preserve the completed cakes. The cakes, in fact, improve as they ripen in the refrigerator over several days and may be frozen without impairment to the flavor or texture. They benefit from a 20- to 30-minute waiting period at room temperature before serving.

Europeans traditionally saturate Génoise with syrup for a very moist cake. Americans favor less syrup.

THE FLOUR/CORNSTARCH MIXTURE
Soft, fine cake flour produces a Génoise with a more velvety crumb than one prepared with all-purpose flour. The added cornstarch tightens the crumb for a moister cake.

Measure the flour by the dip-and-sweep method. Sift it after measuring it and again when adding it to the batter so that the flour doesn't "sit" too heavily on the batter and deflate it.

Be sure to fold all of the flour mixture thoroughly into the batter—any pockets of unincorporated flour will become hard, encapsulated lumps during baking. To facilitate folding, use a perforated skimmer—it provides the proper resistance to incorporate the flour quickly without breaking down the air in the beaten eggs. Your own, slightly cupped hand does a more effective job of folding the flour than a rubber spatula. Fold it gently and rapidly to avoid deflating the eggs.

THE EGGS AND SUGAR
All recipes use large Grade A eggs. Extra-large or jumbo eggs throw off the balance of the recipe. For maximum volume, the eggs must be warm. It is not enough to heat the mixing bowl without heating the eggs, but do not allow the eggs to become hot—they should feel barely warm. Exceptions are the Golden Génoise, where yolks only are used and these should be almost hot, and the Moist Chocolate Génoise, which requires room-temperature eggs for a slightly heavier batter.

The easiest way to heat eggs to lukewarm is to place them unbroken in a mixing bowl and then put the bowl in an unlit gas oven with an automatic pilot light for at least 4 hours or overnight. The pilot light provides just the right amount of heat. When you are ready to prepare the batter, remove the bowl from the oven, crack the warmed eggs directly into it, add the sugar, and beat them immediately to maintain the temperature.

The eggs may also be warmed over simmering water if the egg/sugar mixture is stirred constantly. You may even place the mixing bowl directly on the heat, but great care must be taken not to overheat and cook the eggs.

Warm eggs and sugar should be beaten in an electric mixer on high speed for 5 to 10 minutes, until they are light and fluffy and tripled in volume. The speed is then lowered for 1 minute to deflate the batter slightly and give it body. If the batter is too light, it will rise too much during baking and ultimately collapse. When yolks alone are used, as in the Golden Génoise, a little water should be added to help the batter absorb the flour.

The oven should be preheated, pans prepared and all the ingredients ready and measured before the eggs are beaten. They deflate significantly if they are left standing, which can prove disastrous, because the air beaten into the eggs acts as the leavening agent.

For fine texture, use superfine sugar, available in most supermarkets, or grind granulated sugar in the food processor or blender. As explained earlier (see *Ingredients*, Sugar), it is impossible to overgrind.

BUTTER

Génoise depends on sweet, unsalted butter for its delicate flavor; it is unthinkable to substitute margarine or vegetable shortening. Clarifying the butter produces a richer, purer flavor, because you are eliminating the slightly sour milk solids and water. To clarify butter, simmer it undisturbed until the milk solids begin to turn golden-brown. Remove it from the heat and allow it to stand a few minutes so that the browned particles settle to the bottom. Pour the clear liquid through a fine sieve or cheesecloth.

If you start with 5 tablespoons of butter you will end up with approximately 4 clarified tablespoons. A large amount of butter may be clarified in advance—it keeps well stored in a glass jar in the refrigerator for a few weeks, or months in the freezer. Heat it to lukewarm before adding it to the batter for optimum texture and be sure

to adjust the amount to allow for the fact that the butter is clarified.

Before folding the flour into the batter, remove a small amount of the beaten-eggs-and-sugar mixture and whisk it with the butter. Then fold this mixture into the batter. This guarantees that the butter will blend evenly with the flour in the batter (but does not work if egg yolks only are used, as in Golden Génoise).

THE PAN

Génoise baked in one high pan seems to rise better than when it is baked in two shallow pans, and has an ideal texture. One pan has the added advantage of eliminating two crusts. The crusts must be trimmed, or any added syrup will not be absorbed by the sponge cake. It's an easy matter to slice the baked cake in half for two layers or to cut as many layers as you need (take care to predetermine their depth).

The Génoise recipes here require either a 3-by-8-inch pan or two 1½-by-8-inch pans (for 1½-by-9-inch pans, increase the recipe proportionally, using a total of 6 eggs). Pans with straight sides are best because the cake rises more evenly—it is never higher in the center. The Golden Génoise may also be baked in two heart-shaped flan forms placed on a parchment-lined cookie sheet. The other three Génoise variations also may be baked using flan rings, if desired. The batter should fill the pans or flan forms no less than half and no more than two-thirds; cakes will not rise to the very top of the pan. Line the bottom of a greased pan with parchment or wax paper and then butter and flour the entire inside.

BAKING

Génoise should be baked at 350 degrees on a middle or low oven rack. It is very important not to open the oven door until about 5 minutes before the scheduled end of baking time or the cake may fall.

The cake is done (1) when a cake tester or toothpick comes out of the center clean, (2) when the cake springs back when gently pressed near the center, and (3) when it just barely begins to pull away from the sides of the pan. Remove it from the oven and invert it onto a greased wire rack. Allow the cake to cool for at least an hour.

When cool, use a serrated knife to trim off the top and bottom crusts if you plan to saturate it with syrup. Next, slice it into layers (see *Decorating and Care of the Completed Cake*, Torting). It is easy to lift the layers off each other as the properly baked, cooled cake is quite firm. Brush an equal amount of syrup on both sides of the cake layers for even saturation.

It is preferable to leave the cake intact if you plan to freeze or refrigerate it. Wrap it in plastic wrap and then heavy aluminum foil. It will stay fresh for a month in the freezer, and a week in the refrigerator. Bring the cake to room temperature before slicing and frosting it.

THE RECIPES

The formula for Basic Génoise is devised so that the ingredients are easy to remember and easy to increase and decrease in proportion to the size of your cake pan. See next page for the formula, which can then be multiplied by any number to create a specific recipe. For a 3-by-8-inch cake pan, as I have used, multiply by 5 (it has been done for you in the recipe). For a larger cake pan, increase all measurements proportionally.

Two entirely new versions of the classic Génoise—one Moist Chocolate, the other Golden—follow. Both are downy-soft and feathery-light, yet moist enough to stand on their own without syrup. A Génoise may be used for an infinite variety of desserts: thinly sliced to line a mold; as the base for a soufflé; in a trifle; as *petits fours*; layered and filled with buttercream; or simply dusted with confectioners' sugar.

Formula for Basic Génoise
(all measurements must be multiplied by a common factor to create a recipe)

1 Grade A large egg	1 Grade A large egg
1 ounce sugar	2 tablespoons + 1 teaspoon sugar
1 ounce cake flour/cornstarch mixture	2 tablespoons + 1 teaspoon cake flour + 5 teaspoons cornstarch
½ ounce unsalted butter	1 tablespoon unsalted butter
¼ scant teaspoon vanilla	¼ scant teaspoon vanilla

Basic Génoise

3 ounces (¾ cup) cake flour
2 ounces (½ cup) cornstarch
5 eggs (1 cup)
5 ounces (¾ cup) superfine sugar
2½ ounces (5 tablespoons) unsalted
butter, clarified (4 clarified
tablespoons)
¾ teaspoon vanilla

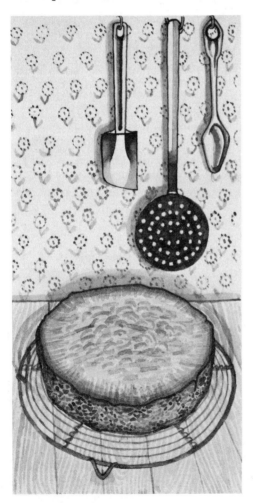

Preheat the oven to 350 degrees. Grease and line the bottom of a 3-by-8-inch cake pan or two 1½-by-8-inch pans. Butter and flour the inside of the pan(s).

Sift the flour and cornstarch together. Set aside.

Place the eggs and sugar in a mixing bowl and heat them over simmering water, whisking constantly, until the mixture is lukewarm. Beat the mixture at the high speed of an electric mixer until it has tripled in volume, about 5 minutes. Lower the speed for 1 minute to add body and to deflate the volume slightly. While the eggs are mixing:

Heat the clarified butter until it is almost hot, 110 to 120 degrees. Add the vanilla to the butter. Remove about 1 cup of the beaten egg/sugar mixture and whisk it into the warmed butter. Set aside.

Sift the flour-cornstarch mixture a second time over the remaining batter in the mixing bowl in two stages, folding after each addition until all the flour has been incorporated. Add the reserved butter mixture and fold it in gently.

Pour the mixture immediately into the prepared pan(s) until two-thirds full. Tap the pan(s) on the counter once or twice to release large air bubbles.

Bake for 35 to 40 minutes if in one pan, 25 to 30 if in two pans, until the cake is golden-brown and begins to pull away slightly from the sides. Do not open the oven door until the cake is almost done, or it may fall.

Run a spatula around the edges and turn out the cake at once onto a greased wire rack. If baked in one pan, the cake will be about 2 to 2½ inches high.

NOTE: This cake needs syrup. For a less airy, moister texture which requires only a sprinkling of liqueur, use 8 tablespoons of butter clarified to about 6½ tablespoons. The resulting cake will not exceed 2 inches in height. You may substitute ¾ cup less 1½ tablespoons of all-purpose flour for cake flour. The texture will vary slightly. Also, you may heat the eggs in the oven, as explained earlier (*The Eggs and Sugar*), instead of over simmering water.

Chocolate Génoise

To make a Chocolate Génoise, replace the ¼ cup of cornstarch with ¼ cup of unsweetened cocoa. Follow the instructions for Basic Génoise. The batter will only half fill the baking pan(s). This cake needs syrup.

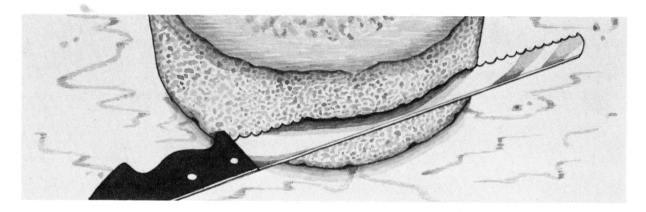

Moist Chocolate Génoise

¼ cup boiling water
5 ounces Tobler extra-bitter-sweet chocolate, or 3 ounces semi-sweet and 2 ounces unsweetened chocolate, chopped
5 eggs at room temperature
5 ounces (¾ cup) superfine sugar
4 ounces (1 cup) cake flour, unsifted
⅛ teaspoon salt

Preheat the oven to 350 degrees. Prepare the cake pan(s) as in the Basic Génoise recipe.

Put the chopped chocolate in a medium-sized bowl and pour the boiling water over it. Stir until the chocolate has melted and is smooth. Cool to lukewarm or room temperature.

Beat the eggs and sugar in a large mixing bowl until the mixture has tripled in volume (about 5 minutes). Sift the flour and salt together, then sift the mixture over the egg/sugar batter in two stages, folding after each addition until the flour disappears.

Drizzle the chocolate onto the batter in two stages, folding after each addition until the color is uniform. Immediately pour the batter into the cake pan(s).

Bake for 45 to 55 minutes, until a cake tester comes out clean and the cake begins to pull away from the sides. Invert the cake at once onto a wire rack.

NOTE: This cake is so moist it does not need syrup. It is very rich and more "chocolatey" than the preceding Chocolate Génoise.

Golden Génoise

Makes 12 servings

3 ounces (¼ cup) cake flour,
  unsifted
1⅓ ounces (⅓ cup) cornstarch,
  unsifted
12 egg yolks
7 ounces (1 cup) superfine sugar
1 teaspoon vanilla
¼ cup water
4 ounces (8 tablespoons) butter,
  clarified and warmed (6½
  clarified tablespoons)

Preheat the oven to 350 degrees. Prepare one 3-by-8-inch pan or two 8¼-inch heart-shaped flan forms on a parchment-lined, buttered and floured baking sheet.

Sift the flour and cornstarch together. Set aside.

Place the yolks and sugar in a large mixing bowl and heat them over simmering water. Do not let the bottom of the bowl touch the water. Whisk constantly but gently until the mixture is almost hot. Beat the mixture in an electric mixer until it is very thick and light-colored, and the bowl is cool (about 5 minutes). Lower the speed and beat in the vanilla and water.

Sift the flour-cornstarch mixture a second time over the batter in two stages, folding after each addition until all the flour has been incorporated. Warm the butter and fold it in gently in two stages. Immediately pour the batter into the prepared pan(s).

Bake for 40 to 45 minutes if in one pan, 20 minutes if in heart-shaped flan forms. The cake will be pale golden when baked, not browned. Invert the cake at once onto a wire rack. The cake will sink slightly.

NOTE: This cake is so moist it does not need syrup. It has a crunchy, meringue-like crust and is delicious to eat plain. After having been frozen for several weeks it still retains a fresh-baked quality if it is brought to room temperature.

Gâteau au Grand Marnier et Chocolat

This cake is downy-soft and moist without a trace of wetness. The Grand Marnier both perfumes and preserves. The cake was developed as an annual birthday present for my brother who lives in California. Every year the birthday card always included a note to please be sure and let me know how the cake survived the trip. Every year for three years my brother informed me that it had survived perfectly until the fourth year when he changed his comment to: "This time it was really *perfect." It turned out that the three first tries had always broken into a few pieces, but he had been afraid to tell me because he loved even the crumbs so much and, knowing my penchant for perfectionism, was afraid that if I knew the cake was less than perfect I would stop sending it! The solution to the breaking problem was to reduce the mixing time for the batter.*

Once I felt the cake had been perfected I was ready for the ultimate test: to send it to a friend in France (first-class, of course). My friend Jean-Pierre swears it arrived in perfect condition, and needed only a fresh chocolate glaze, but can I believe him?

BATTER:

8¾ ounces (2½ cups) sifted cake flour

1½ teaspoons baking powder

1 teaspoon baking soda

¼ teaspoon salt

½ pound (16 tablespoons) unsalted butter (softened)

6¾ ounces (1 cup) sugar

4 eggs

1 cup sour cream

½ cup blanched almonds, chopped fine but not powder-fine, mixed with 2 tablespoons grated orange rind

½ cup semi-sweet chocolate bits (mini) or coarsely grated Tobler, extra-bitter-sweet chocolate

¼ teaspoon Grand Marnier (optional)

½ tablespoon flour

GLAZE 1:

Grand Marnier orange-juice syrup (see page 72)

GLAZE 2 (optional):

½ recipe for Ganache Glaze using Grand Marnier (see page 81)

Preheat the oven to 325 degrees. Grease and flour a 3½-by-9-inch (9-cup) tube pan or Kugelhopf pan.

Place the flour, baking powder, baking soda and salt in a medium-sized bowl. Using a wire whisk or fork, stir to blend the ingredients well.

Beat the softened butter in a large mixing bowl until it is light; add the sugar and continue beating until the mixture is fluffy (about 4 minutes on medium speed). Beat in the eggs, one at a time, until each is well incorporated.

With the mixer on low speed, add the flour mixture in thirds, alternating with the sour cream and beating in each addition only until it is uniformly incorporated. Stir in the orange rind and nuts, and set aside for a few moments.

Place the chocolate bits in a small bowl, and sprinkle them with Grand Marnier, tossing lightly with a rubber spatula or spoon to coat them. Add the flour and toss them again until the bits are coated. Shake off any excess flour in a strainer and gently fold the bits into the batter. Pour or spoon the batter into the prepared pan and bake 55 to 65 minutes or until a cake tester inserted toward the middle comes out clean and the cake springs back when it is gently pressed with a finger tip.

While the cake is baking, prepare Glaze 1.

When the cake is done, remove it from the oven and prick the top all over with a fork. Brush on about one-half of the glaze, using a pastry brush or a small spoon. Place the pan on a rack and allow it to cool for 10 minutes. Unmold the cake onto the rack, and brush on the remaining glaze. Allow

the cake to cool to room temperature (about 1 hour) and place it on a serving plate or cake stand. Pour on Glaze 2 if desired.

NOTE: Store the cake at room temperature. If it is tightly wrapped, it will remain freshly moist for at least a week and may be kept even up to 3 weeks. (If you are using the Ganache Glaze, the cake should be refrigerated after a week.)

Chocolate Cloud Roll

Makes 10-12 servings

This chocolate roll manages to be fudgy and ethereal at the same time. It is best eaten the same day it is made, but it will keep admirably for one to two days in the refrigerator.

4 ounces Tobler extra-bitter-sweet or bitter-sweet chocolate
6 eggs separated, at room temperature
6¾ ounces (1 cup) sugar
Pinch of salt
⅕ ounce (1 tablespoon) cocoa
1 cup heavy cream
2 tablespoons confectioners' sugar

GLAZE:
Ganache (½ recipe using Kahlua) (see page 81)

Adjust the oven rack one-third up from the bottom of the oven and preheat the oven to 350 degrees.

Melt the bitter-sweet chocolate in a small heavy saucepan or the top of a double boiler over hot water; set aside to cool.

Grease an 11-by-17-inch or a 10½-by-15½-inch jelly-roll pan with ½ tablespoon vegetable shortening, and line the pan with parchment or wax paper allowing this to extend slightly over the short edges for ease in removal. Oil the top side of the wax paper with ½ tablespoon oil, and dust it with fine, dry breadcrumbs.

Beat the egg yolks with ¾ cup sugar in a small mixing bowl, with the mixer on high speed, for about 5 minutes or until the mixture is fluffy and pale yellow. Blend the melted chocolate into the egg yolks, on low speed.

Beat the egg whites with the pinch of salt in a large mixing bowl until soft peaks form. Gradually add the remaining ¼ cup granulated sugar, beating only until stiff peaks form.

Gently stir one-fourth of the egg whites into the chocolate mixture to lighten it. Then fold in the remaining whites until just blended. Pour the mixture into the prepared pan, spreading gently and evenly with a spatula. Bake for 18 minutes. The cake will have puffed and lost its shine, and a cake tester will come out clean, but the cake will not spring back when touched with a finger. It is extremely important not to overbake and dry out the cake or it will not be moist and fudgy and will not roll well.

Wet a clean dish towel and wring it out well. Remove the cake from the oven, leaving it in the pan to cool, and cover it immediately with the damp towel. Allow the cake to cool to room temperature. Uncover it and dust it lightly with cocoa. Invert it onto the same towel. Carefully peel off the wax paper and discard it.

Beat the heavy cream and confectioners' sugar on high speed just until peaks form, and spread it onto the cake. Roll the cake in jelly-roll fashion from the longer side. Roll it onto a cookie sheet or long serving platter, removing the towel. If it appears that the final roll will land seam-side up, roll it onto a long strip of foil and then onto the serving platter. Decorate it with Ganache Glaze poured zig-zag down the center of the roll. Refrigerate it until serving time.

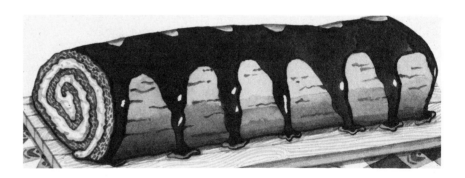

Triple Chocolate Proposal Cake

Makes 14-16 small, rich servings

This cake has three different sensations, all of them intensely chocolate: the cake is moist and light; the filling rich and creamy; and the topping crisp and crunchy.

The cake is named "triple" not only because of its three chocolate components but because I have received three proposals of marriage as a result of it. The first came from a happily married woman, the second from a man at a party who had eaten the cake but not yet met me, and the third from my husband, who doesn't love the cake but who married me anyway!

CAKE:
3-ounce bar Tobler extra-bitter-sweet chocolate
1-ounce square unsweetened chocolate (or substitute 2 ounces semi-sweet and 2 ounces unsweetened chocolate)
1 cup water
4 eggs at room temperature
4¾ ounces (⅔ cup) superfine sugar
3 ounces (¾ cup) unsifted cake flour
⅛ teaspoon salt

Preheat the oven to 350 degrees.

Lightly grease the bottom of a 3-by-9-inch cake pan or a 9-inch springform and line it with wax paper or parchment. (There is no need to grease the bottom if you are using parchment.)

Place the chocolate and water in a small, heavy saucepan over low heat, and bring to a boil, stirring constantly to melt the chocolate. Simmer for 3 to 4 minutes; the mixture will thicken slightly and resemble unwhipped heavy cream. Cool to lukewarm or cool. (It will measure about 1⅓ cups.)

Place the eggs and sugar in the large bowl of an electric mixer, and beat them on high speed for 5 to 10 minutes, scraping the sides of the bowl once or twice. The mixture will be thick, pale yellow and greatly increased in volume.

While the eggs are beating, sift together the flour and salt onto a piece of wax paper. Sift again into the egg mixture using a whisk to fold in, just until all the flour disappears and is incorporated.

Drizzle the cooled chocolate onto the batter in two stages, folding it in until the batter is uniform in color. Pour the batter into the pan (which should be two-thirds full) and tap it on the counter once or twice to free any large air bubbles. Bake 70 minutes. Cracks will appear on the surface and the cake tester, when inserted in the center, will enter almost as easily as when it is inserted toward the sides. (The cake will start to shrink from the sides of the pan long before it is done.) Run a small, sharp knife or metal spatula between the sides of the cake and pan to be sure all the sides are free and invert the cake onto a lightly greased rack. Remove the bottom of the pan, if springform, and parchment. Allow the cake to cool completely—at least 1 hour. The cake will fall slightly in the center. The overall height will be about 1½ inches.

If the cake falls more, it was underbaked, but it will still taste delicious. Slice into two layers.

Ganache is used for both filling and frosting this cake (see under *Light Ganache.* Use double the recipe.)

Decorate the top with Praline Leaves (recipe follows).

PRALINE LEAVES

Do not make praline on a humid day.

The chocolate must be tempered for consistent results. (See Chocolate Tempering, page 16.)

2½ ounces (½ cup) filberts (hazelnuts), peeled (see page 12)
3½ ounces (½ cup) sugar
2 tablespoons water
4 ounces Tobler extra-bitter-sweet chocolate (or 3 ounces semi-sweet and 1 ounce unsweetened)

Bake the filberts in a 350-degree oven for about 20 minutes or until the nuts brown lightly. Place them on a nonstick cookie sheet or a 12-inch square of lightly oiled heavy-duty foil.

Combine the sugar and water in a small, heavy saucepan, and cook over medium heat, stirring constantly until the sugar is dissolved. Increase the heat to medium-high and allow to boil undisturbed until the sugar begins to caramelize. (It will begin to look like dark corn syrup and take on the characteristic smell of caramel or "burnt sugar." Immediately pour the caramel over the nuts. Allow to cool and harden (about 15 to 20 minutes). Remove from the sheet and break into a few pieces. Grind in the food processor until finely powdered. Temper the chocolate to 89 to 91 degrees, and stir in the powdered nut mixture until smooth.

Pour the chocolate mixture in a long line down the center of a 36-inch strip of wax paper. Cover it with a second strip and roll it into a large rectangle about 11 by 30 inches, making the surface as smooth and ripple-free as possible. Allow

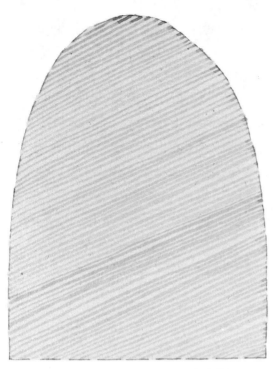

TEMPLATE FOR PRALINE LEAVES
(trace exact size)

it to set for 10 to 15 minutes and then, with scissors, cut it into three 10-inch pieces. Stack them on a cookie sheet and refrigerate. If the chocolate was tempered correctly, it will harden in 15 minutes.

When the chocolate is firm, peel off both sides of the wax paper and store the chocolate pieces at room temperature until you are ready to use them. They will keep for several weeks at room temperature, but are easier to cut into shape when first made. If they harden and the shapes crack, use a hair dryer waved briefly over the surface to soften it slightly without actually melting it.

Measure the diameter of the cake and cut one chocolate circle to use as the top. Trace the outline of the template at left and use it to cut petals (you will need about 14).

Assembling Cake:
Invert the cake onto a serving plate (covered with a doily, if desired). Slip 4 strips of wax paper under the edges of the cake to protect the surface. Using a sharp knife, preferably serrated, cut the cake into 2 layers. Remove the top layer, using a wide spatula or an open-ended cookie sheet. Sandwich the layers with about 1 cup of Ganache. Smoothly frost the top and sides of the cake, reserving at least a cup to attach the chocolate petals.

Using a wide spatula, carefully transfer the large chocolate circle to the top of the cake. If the chocolate seems a bit flexible, chill it for a few minutes before placing it on the cake. Surround the cake with slightly overlapping chocolate petals, using the Ganache as necessary to secure them. To curve the petals slightly inward, wave a hair dryer at them briefly from a few inches away but be careful to stop before the chocolate darkens and begins to melt. Then press gently against the tips of the petals.

If desired, encircle the bottom of the petals with a wide, satin ribbon and place a chocolate or pale-pink marzipan or a fresh rose with 2 chocolate leaves on top. This is a very easy way to decorate with praline leaves. For a greater challenge, double the praline leaves' ingredients and spoon approximately equal amounts of the mixture onto six 12-inch squares of wax paper. Cover each with another sheet of wax paper and, with a rolling pin, smooth them into thin, flat,

rectangular sheets with rounded corners. When they are firm, peel off the wax paper but use it to transport the chocolate sheets to the cake. Press one long edge against the side of the cake, bending the leaf in a slight arch. Gently remove the wax paper. Do the same with the remaining 5 leaves, overlapping and gently molding them to shape. When they are all in place, use a hair dryer, if necessary, to make the leaves pliable enough to drape into interesting configurations without cracking. Sprinkle them lightly with confectioners' sugar.

NOTE: Chocolate is sensitive to changes in temperature and humidity. If you do not temper the chocolate, the leaves will sometimes soften and become wet-looking even though they were quite firm in the refrigerator. If left uncovered at room temperature, they will usually harden overnight. To further coax them into submission, they can also be gently remelted in the top of a double boiler over hot water to 92 degrees and then re-rolled with a good chance of success.

TO SERVE: Remove the cake from the refrigerator 30 minutes before serving. Cut it with a thin, sharp knife that has been dipped in hot water and dried. The cake freezes exceptionally well for 3 to 4 months. To freeze, place it in the freezer, uncovered, until it is firm and then wrap it carefully with heavy-duty foil.

Le Gâteau Tombé *(The Fallen Cake)*

This cake was created, naturally, by accident. It is a perfect example of how a new concept and a French name can turn a disaster into a spectacular new dessert. It uses the same recipe as the Triple Chocolate Proposal Cake but the eggs and sugar are first warmed as for a Génoise. This results in too much volume for the structure of the cake to support and causes the center to collapse, leaving a nice-sized crater to receive whipped cream and chocolate curls, Tart Cherry Topping (page 72), or whatever you desire.

Use a 3-by-8-inch pan and bake at 350 degrees for 60 to 70 minutes. Cool the cake in the pan for 10 to 20 minutes before unmolding it onto a greased rack. Reinvert it at once onto a second greased rack so that the top side with the crater remains up.

Passover Variation

I often make the Triple Chocolate Proposal Cake for our family seder using a nut torte in place of the cake part. Although it is not considered strictly kosher because of the cream (which is not allowed after a meat meal) and Tobler chocolate, which is by no means "kosher for Passover," I feel it fulfills the most important criterion—it contains no flour. My family will accept a lot, but flour at Passover time would definitely be going too far!

8 ounces (½ pound) (16 tablespoons) butter

7 ounces (1 cup) superfine sugar

8 eggs, separated

8 ounces Tobler extra-bitter-sweet chocolate (or 6 ounces semi-sweet and 2 ounces unsweetened), melted and cooled

8 ounces (1⅔ cup) peeled, ground hazelnuts or almonds

¼ teaspoon salt

Preheat the oven to 350 degrees.

Thoroughly grease the bottoms of two 1½-by-9-inch pans, then line them with parchment.

Cream the butter and all but 2 tablespoons of the sugar in the large bowl of an electric mixer on medium-high speed for about 3 minutes or until the mixture is light and fluffy. Add the egg yolks, one at a time, beating well after each addition. On low speed, beat in the cool, melted chocolate, then the ground nuts.

If the mixer has only one bowl, scrape this mixture into another large bowl or container. Wash the mixing bowl and beater well and beat the egg whites with the ¼ teaspoon salt until soft peaks form. Gradually add the remaining 2 tablespoons of sugar and beat only until stiff peaks form. Stir about a quarter of the beaten whites into the chocolate mixture to lighten it. Then gently fold in the remaining whites. Pour the mixture into the pans and bake 55 to 60 minutes. Cool the cakes in the pans until they are just warm (about 45 minutes) and run a small metal spatula around the sides before inverting them onto a greased rack to finish cooling. Sandwich the 2 layers with Ganache filling and proceed as for Triple Chocolate Proposal Cake.

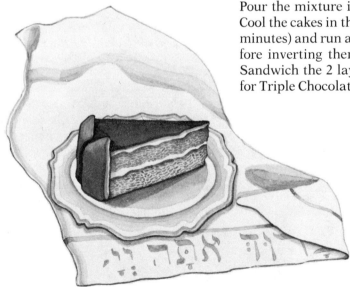

Chocolate Soufflé Ray

The basis for this extraordinary recipe was given to me by a student named Ray who promised me the lightest, moistest chocolate cake I ever tasted. We were both surprised to discover that the "cake" was a soufflé and that, fallen and cold, it could also double as a cake. Ray is now chef-owner of Restaurant Rosasco in Mendocino, California.

4 eggs, separated
2 ounces Tobler extra-bitter-sweet
   chocolate, melted
2 ounces (4 tablespoons) butter,
   clarified (will be about
   3 tablespoons)
3 ounces (6 tablespoons) water
1 tablespoon flour (optional,
   see Note)
2⅛ ounces (5 tablespoons) sugar
1 tablespoon brandy
Pinch of salt

Preheat the oven to 350 degrees (convection 300 degrees).

Butter and sugar a 3-inch-high foil collar and tie it to a 4- to 5-cup soufflé mold. Butter and sugar the mold. Or grease and flour a 1½-by-9-inch cake pan or line it with parchment.

Combine the yolks, melted chocolate, melted butter and water in a small heavy saucepan or the top of a double boiler.

Caramelize 4 tablespoons of the sugar dissolved in 2 tablespoons water in a small heavy saucepan. Whisk the very hot caramel into the chocolate mixture until it is smooth and all lumps are dissolved. Allow the mixture to cool until it is no longer hot. Add the brandy and set aside.

Beat the whites with the pinch of salt until soft peaks form. Gradually beat in the remaining 1 tablespoon of sugar until almost stiff peaks form. Stir about ½ cup of the beaten whites into the chocolate mixture and fold in the remainder. Pour the mixture into the prepared mold and bake 30 to 35 minutes until a knife inserted (quickly) in the center comes out clean. Remove it from the oven and dust it lightly with confectioners' sugar, if desired. Serve at once. (For a cake, bake 30 to 40 minutes or until a cake tester inserted in the center comes out clean. Cool it in the pan for 30 minutes and invert it onto a greased rack to cool.)

For soufflé: serve with warm Ganache Glaze.

For cake: sprinkle lightly with confectioners' sugar.

NOTE: If desired, add 1 tablespoon of flour to the egg yolk mixture. It will thicken the mixture slightly, making it easier to fold into the whites, but does not affect the texture.

Introduction to Puff Pastry

Puff the Magic Pastry

Puff pastry is composed of alternate layers of dough and fat, created by folding the dough, which are referred to as "turns." Gluten, found in greater quantities in hard wheat than ordinary flour, plays an important role in the pastry's ability to puff. Gluten is made up of one part protein and two parts water. On heating, the water turns to steam, thus creating a great deal of pressure within the gluten structure, causing it to rise.

Puff pastry works best in cool, dry weather, because when the fat becomes too warm, it melts and breaks through the dough layers. The best-*tasting* puff pastry is made with butter. However, the best-*textured* puff pastry is achieved with vegetable shortening. Butter with a low water content is highly desirable, because too much water will toughen the gluten. (An excess of water may appear as spots on the surface of the final product.)

How to Use Puff Pastry

The primary use for puff pastry in cake making is as a component of such classics as the Gâteau St. Honoré (page 53). It also can serve as crust for fruit or cream pies and tarts. One of its most appealing forms is the small patty shell known as *vol-au-vent* ("fly with the wind"), in which a tiny cap is perched atop a filling of chilled pastry cream and fresh fruit. The vol-au-vent can be shaped ahead, and frozen—pastry cream also freezes well. If the shells are brushed with apricot glaze or caramel they may be filled with pastry cream several hours in advance, as the glaze keeps them from getting soggy.

Any leftovers can be made into savory pastries, hors d'oeuvres or cheese straws. Traditionally, puff pastry is served hot only in its savory forms.

Rolling Out Dough

Marble is the preferred surface for working with puff pastry, because it maintains a cool temperature, but oilcloth, formica or wood are fine. If the pastry starts to soften you should quickly slide it onto a flat baking sheet, cover it with plastic wrap, and refrigerate it for about 30 minutes, or until it is firm and cool again.

The work surface should be lightly dusted with flour to prevent sticking, and a small amount of flour rubbed lightly into the surface of the pastry. Always roll puff pastry into a square or rectangular shape, regardless of the final shape desired. Decrease the pressure toward the edge to avoid flattening the edge and squeezing the layers together. Evenness of rolling is essential for even rising. A heavy rolling pin is an asset.

A *tutove* rolling pin is specially designed for

rolling puff pastry. It is covered with rounded ridges, which help to distribute the butter evenly without breaking through the pastry. A long, heavy rolling pin is also a great help, because it alleviates the need to press forcefully when rolling out the pastry.

RESTING AND RELAXATION *(of pastry!)*
The gluten in pastry causes it to shrink or spring back when rolled. It is therefore important to rest puff pastry after shaping it. The ideal is to refrigerate it (covered to avoid drying, because moisture is important to its rise) 6 hours to overnight and up to 1½ days before baking. Next best would be to bake it from a thoroughly frozen state or partially frozen for 30 minutes to 1 hour in the freezer (wrapped airtight). But be sure to let it relax before freezing. At the very least, it should be refrigerated for 30 minutes to 1 hour.

SHAPING
When cutting the pastry, the object is to create edges that will leave the layers of pastry open and able to rise freely, as opposed to edges that are stuck together or closed. To accomplish this, always use a sharp knife with an up/down motion as opposed to a dragging motion, or use an unfloured biscuit cutter pressed firmly down, straight through the pastry. Do not twist the cutter, and be sure to wipe it clean after each cut. Never use an uncut edge of puff pastry, because the layers will be closed and sealed.

To attach one piece of puff pastry to another, use an egg wash made from one yolk lightly beaten with one teaspoon water. This acts as glue, so it is important that it be applied carefully and not allowed to drip onto the sides, sealing them shut. *Never* pinch the edges together. Only press lightly from the top surface. The same egg wash can be used as a glaze. It should be applied just before baking; a second coat can be applied after one minute.

BAKING SHEETS
Avoid nonstick and black-bottomed baking sheets when baking puff pastry. When used in gas nonconvection ovens, the black-bottomed baking sheets tend to create the same effect on the bottoms of the pastries, and the nonstick surface does not provide the necessary traction to enable the puff pastry to rise to its best advantage. A heavy baking sheet lined with parchment or brushed with water is best. Pastries should be placed about one inch apart.

STORAGE
Puff pastry can be kept frozen for up to 1 year in a good freezer (one which maintains close to zero degrees). It can also be refrozen twice after its initial freezing without any significant loss in rising ability. This is particularly useful for make-ahead hors d'oeuvres—the dough can be rolled, stuffed, shaped and refrozen until shortly before serving time. In fact, puff pastry bakes best from the frozen state, because the contrast from very cold to very hot gives it an added shock, or boost, on its way up! It also tends to bake more evenly and with less shrinkage.

Once pastry is defrosted, it should not remain in the refrigerator for more than 2 days. If it cannot be used by then, it is better to refreeze it.

DEFROSTING
Frozen puff pastry will defrost in 4 hours to overnight in the refrigerator or in 1 to 2 hours at room temperature. It should still be cool but malleable enough to roll smoothly. Do not roll it if it is stiff, partly frozen or too hard.

To defrost only part of a piece of frozen pastry, use a serrated knife and make a quarter-inch-deep cut the length of the size of piece desired. Then strike the pastry sharply on the edge of a table top or counter, along the underneath side of the cut, and the piece will break off cleanly.

BAKING

Puff pastry baked in a convection-type oven browns beautifully and evenly with no excess browning of the base. Four-inch vol-au-vents take about 15 minutes at 400 degrees (preheated 5 minutes). In a conventional oven, it is best to place the pastry in the upper third of the oven to avoid overbrowning the bases.

In a conventional oven, bake vol-au-vents at a preheated 450 degrees for 10 minutes, then at 350 degrees for 10 to 15 minutes more for small ones and 15 to 20 minutes more for large ones, or until they are golden-brown. To make beautifully even vol-au-vents, check them after 4 minutes of baking (8 minutes if baked from the frozen state). They will just be beginning to puff up—no dramatic rise will have taken place yet but you will be able to see which part (or parts) is rising higher than the rest. Using a small, sharp knife, insert it quickly about half an inch into the edge of the rim—not the rim itself—in front of the higher part. This will release the steam and cause the higher part to level off. It will continue to rise evenly. Do this procedure as quickly as possible so that heat from the oven does not escape.

Another technique used to make a perfectly even vol-au-vent is to suspend a rack about 2 inches over the vol-au-vent, using pyrex cups or other 2-inch objects as supports. If one side of the vol-au-vent rises faster than the rest, it hits the rack and levels out instead of toppling over.

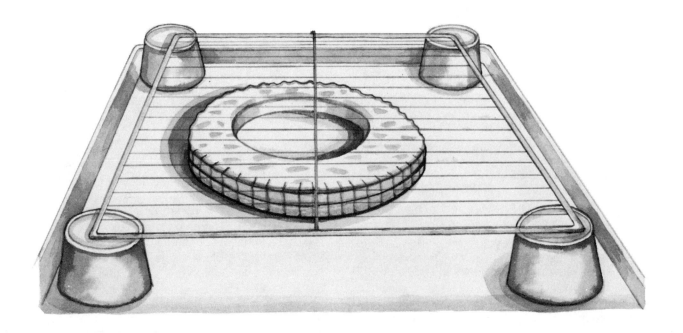

The Best of All Possible Puff Pastries

Makes 2½ pounds

There are many acceptable ways to make puff pastry, and I feel as though I have tried close to all of them. The reason I prefer this puff pastry to all the countless other versions is that it is exceptionally crisp and tender. This is due to the initial undermanipulation of the détrempe *(dough). The gluten in the pastry gets adequately activated on subsequent rollings—you will find you need to let it rest after the first two turns.*

In this method of making puff pastry, about 14 percent of the flour is mixed with the butter to form a square "package" and about 14 percent of the butter is mixed with the flour and water to produce a soft dough (the détrempe*), which encases the butter package.*

Notice that there is equal weight of butter and flour, and that a quarter of their combined weight is water. This recipe may be increased or decreased as needed.

1 pound butter
1 pound (3⅔ cups) unbleached all-
purpose flour (such as Heckers)
⅓ ounce (1½ teaspoons) salt
¼ ounce (1½ teaspoons) sugar
½ pound (1 cup) cold (not iced)
water

Remove the butter from the refrigerator.

Place the flour in a mixing bowl reserving ½ cup (2 ounces) for the butter package. Add 4 tablespoons (2 ounces) of the butter, the salt and sugar, and rub the mixture between the palms of your hand or fingers until it is very fine and grainy and no lumps of butter are discernible (about 5 minutes). Add ¾ cup of the water and shake the bowl to mix and form soft curds. Mix very gently with a rubber spatula and add the remaining water by droplets, only as much as needed to moisten any loose flour. The dough should be soft and ropey and not smooth and elastic. Dump it out onto a floured surface and squeeze it gently together. Do not try to make a ball. Cover it with a dry cloth.

The Butter:

Put the remaining butter and the reserved ½ cup flour into a zip-lock bag and pound it with a rolling pin to soften it uniformly. Knead it with the heel of your hand until the butter is malleable but remains cold. Form it into a flattish square of about 5 inches.

Uncover the dough, flour it lightly and pat it gently into about an 8-inch square. Place the butter diagonally in the center of the dough square and lightly mark the dough at the edges of the butter with the dull side of a knife. Remove the butter and roll each marked corner of the dough to half its thickness. Moisten the corners lightly with water and replace the butter on the dough and wrap it securely. Turn the dough package over and pound it with the rolling pin to form a flat rectangle, keeping the edges even.

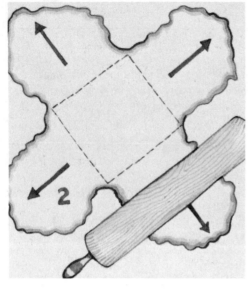

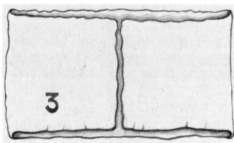

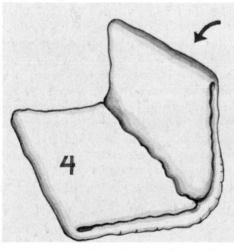

Roll the dough to about a 7-by-15-inch rectangle, dusting the work surface and the dough lightly with flour and moving the dough between every few rollings to be sure it is not sticking. If any breakthrough of butter should occur, rub lightly with flour, and if the butter seems to be softening, slide the dough onto a cookie sheet and chill it until it firms up a bit.

To prevent distortion of the dough during baking, be sure to roll it in all four directions and into its corners, keeping sides even.

Brush off any excess flour on the surface of the dough (to prevent toughness) and make the first double turn. (Bring the short edges to the center and then fold the dough in half.) Turn the dough so that the closed end is facing to your left. Pound the dough again with the rolling pin to flatten it and roll it a second time to the same-sized rectangle. Give the dough a second double turn, continuing to flour and move the dough as needed, and brushing off the excess flour before the turn. Wrap the dough well with foil or plastic wrap and refrigerate it for at least 2 hours to chill the butter and relax the gluten.

Remove the dough from the refrigerator and, if it is very hard, allow it to sit at room temperature until the dough softens enough to pound with a rolling pin without it cracking. Give the dough two more double turns. (If using as a base for a Gâteau St. Honoré, one more turn is sufficient.) For vol-au-vents, where a very high puff is desirable, give it the two turns.

Wrap the dough well and refrigerate it at least 2 hours before the final rolling and shaping.

NOTE: I prefer to let the dough rest overnight (refrigerated) after shaping. The dough will remain fresh for about 3 days in the refrigerator. The older the dough, the less the distortion takes place during baking and also the less the rise. This is mainly because the dough loses moisture as it ages.

When flakiness is desired but a high rise is not, the pastry is sometimes docked (pricked with sharp tines) all over the surface so the steam will escape instead of making the pastry rise. I find this tends to toughen the pastry, and I prefer to roll it extra thin to achieve the same effect. The dough, however, must be adequately relaxed or it is virtually impossible to roll it thin.

Bake as directed on page 48.

½ recipe puff pastry

½ recipe puff pastry

LARGE VOL-AU-VENT
Makes one 12-inch shell

With most puff pastry there will be some degree of shrinkage, so start out with a circle ½ to 1 inch larger than desired. This amount of puff pastry can be rolled to a 12-inch square about ¼ inch thick. Transfer it to a parchment-lined baking sheet (or brush the baking sheet with water) at this point because, once cut, it will be very difficult to transfer without deforming it and even the slightest irregularity becomes magnified after rising. Using a lid, cake pan or other round object, cut a 12-inch circle. Reserve the cutaway edges for another use. To form the rim of the patty, cut a ¾-inch circular strip from the edge of the circle. Brush a ¾-inch egg wash around the border of the circle. Cut through the circular strip to open it and arrange it on top of the egg-wash border so that the edges of the strip and circle are even. Cut off the excess from the strip so that the ends overlap only slightly and attach the overlap with egg wash. Press gently all along the top of the strip. With a fork, prick the center of the circle up to the rim to prevent uneven rising. Cover it with plastic wrap and chill it for at least 1 hour. Apply the egg wash as glaze if desired, or brush it lightly with cold water. (The water will create steam, which also aids the rising process.)

Bake as directed on page 48.

SMALL VOL-AU-VENT
Makes 8 shells and covers

Roll pastry into a 12-inch square, ¼ inch thick (³⁄₁₆ inch thick is also fine for small patties). With a 4-inch biscuit cutter, cut 8 circles. Using a 3½-inch biscuit cutter, cut out the centers of 4 of these circles and, using egg wash to adhere them, place the resulting rims on the remaining 4 circles. (Use the centers as covers if desired.) Prick the centers up to the rim and prick the covers to prevent shrinkage. Transfer them to a prepared baking sheet, using a wide spatula and being careful not to alter their shape.

Bake as directed on page 48.

Pâte Brisée *(Pastry Dough)*

Makes 1 shell and lattice

The food processor produces an excellent and speedy pastry dough provided that the dough does not get over-worked or overblended. This recipe may be prepared by conventional methods as well. (Use double the recipe for double crust pie or two tart shells.)

1⅓ cup flour
¼ pound (1 stick—8 tablespoons)
  cold, sweet butter cut into pieces
½ teaspoon salt
3-4 tablespoons ice water

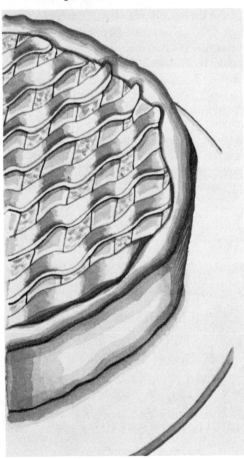

Using metal blade, process all ingredients except water for about 9 seconds or until the mixture looks like coarse meal. Remove cover from work bowl and sprinkle 3 tablespoons ice water all over surface of mixture. Process only until dough begins to hold together. Do not wait until the mixture forms a ball. If after 4 seconds, dough does not begin to mass, add remaining water. Dump out onto work surface or plastic wrap and gently squeeze together to form a flattened ball. Use at once or chill before rolling out.

Baking:
For large, prebaked pastry shell, chill shell, line with foil and fill with pie weights or beans. Bake at 425 degrees for 15 to 20 minutes. Remove foil and weights, prick well with fork and continue baking about 5 minutes or until pale golden-brown.

If mixing by hand, use half butter and half margarine for ease in handling.

NOTE: Copper pennies (while they're still around) make wonderful pie weights, because copper is such an unequaled conductor of heat. Oddly enough, they are less expensive than aluminum pie weights. I find that plastic wrap works very well for rolling out pie crusts. Waxed paper usually wrinkles, but if you wet the counter surface slightly, it helps a lot. I roll out the crust between 2 sheets of either plastic wrap or wax paper.

For small tartlets allow the dough to form a ball. This additional mixing produces a dough that is slightly less flaky and will not puff out of shape in tiny molds where the use of weights would be inconvenient. Bake at 425 degrees for about 10 minutes or until pale golden-brown. Unmold as soon as removed from oven.

Gâteau St. Honoré

Gâteau St. Honoré is a spectacular and dramatic finale to a meal, combining five of the most important techniques in dessert making:

Pâte feuillettée *(puff pastry) or* pâte brisée *(pastry)*
Pâte à chou *(cream puff pastry)*
Crème patissière St. Honoré
Caramel
Spun sugar (angel's hair)

PASTRY

For the base you will need one baked pastry round 8 to 9½ inches in diameter, preferably puff pastry. As it will shrink while baking, cut out a 9½- to 10-inch round of pastry, place it on a wet baking sheet and, to level the surface, top it with a lightly oiled cake pan of equal or larger diameter. Evenly distribute metal weights or beans in the pan as additional weight. Remove the pan toward the end of cooking to allow the pastry to brown lightly. (Bake in a 400-degree oven for about 20 to 30 minutes. Cut a small wedge in center to make sure dough is fully cooked.)

PÂTE À CHOU

½ cup milk
½ cup water
4 ounces (8 tablespoons) butter, cut into pieces or softened to room temperature
1 teaspoon sugar
½ teaspoon salt
4½ ounces (1 cup) flour
5 eggs (1 cup)

Combine the milk, water, butter, sugar and salt in a saucepan, and bring the mixture to a full boil. Remove the saucepan immediately from the heat and add all of the flour at once. Stir with a wooden spoon until the mixture forms a ball, leaves the sides of the pan and clings slightly to the spoon. Return to low heat and cook, stirring and mashing continuously for 3 to 5 minutes to cook the flour. Do not scrape the pan, but transfer the mixture to the large bowl of an electric mixer and cool it for 5 minutes.

Add the eggs, one at a time, beating after each addition until they are incorporated. To insure even puffing do not overbeat after the last addition. The batter will be smooth, shiny and just barely thick enough to hold a very soft peak when lifted. If it is too stiff a little more egg may be added, which will improve the rising, but the batter must be stiff enough to hold its shape for piping.

The mixture may be refrigerated overnight, but should be beaten lightly with a wooden spoon before use.

TIPS:

Water instead of milk makes a lighter puff.

Margarine instead of butter also makes a lighter puff. (The milk and butter contribute flavor.)

Spray or brush the baking sheets with water, and the steam created will help the puffs to rise.

The food processor does a wonderful job with *pâte à chou*. After cooking the flour for 3 to 5 minutes, transfer the "dough" into a processor container with a metal blade. Leave the feed tube open and process the dough for 15 seconds. This will help to cool it slightly. With the processor running, add the eggs and process for another 30 seconds or until the dough is smooth and elastic.

Forming and Baking Chou

Measure the baked pastry round and cut a piece of wax paper or parchment the same diameter. Attach the paper to the baking sheet using a bit of the *pâte à chou* mixture as an adhesive. Fill the pastry bag and, using a ½-inch tip or coupler without a tip, pipe a circle just inside the edge of the paper for a halo. (Leave a small margin because the *chou* expands during baking.) Cut off the end of the circle with a wet spatula. Pipe a curlicue inside the circle and then pipe individual puffs 1½ inches in diameter about 1 inch apart. To ensure a smooth top, smooth away any peaks that form with a wet finger or spatula. You will need 14 to 16 puffs. This recipe makes enough for about 28 puffs in addition to the halo and curlicue.

Bake at 425 degrees for 10 minutes; lower to 350 degrees and bake for 15 to 20 minutes; when the puffs are golden, turn off the oven and remove them to a rack. Make a small slit in the bottoms to release steam. Return them to the turned-off oven, still on the rack, and use a wooden spoon to keep the oven door slightly ajar for 10 minutes. Then close the oven door and leave the puffs in the oven for 1½ hours to dry out completely. If you are planning to freeze the puffs, omit the 1½ hours drying and, when you are ready to use them, defrost for 24 hours in the refrigerator and place them in a 150-degree oven for 1½ hours.

Cool the puffs and store them in an airtight plastic bag or container. They may be stored in the refrigerator for 1 week.

To recrisp, place them in a 350-degree oven for 10 to 15 minutes. Cool them before filling.

NOTE: If a layer of moist dough remains in the center, the entire puff will become soggy on standing.

CRÈME ST. HONORÉ

1½ cups milk
4 egg yolks
3½ ounces (½ cup) sugar
2 tablespoons cornstarch
1-1½ envelopes gelatin
1½ teaspoons vanilla
2 tablespoons Grand Marnier
1½ cups heavy cream

Bring the milk to boiling point in a medium-sized saucepan, and keep it hot. Beat the yolks and sugar in a mixing bowl until the mixture is very thick and pale yellow and a ribbon forms when the beaters are lifted. Add the cornstarch and gelatin (use the larger amount when planning to serve soon after preparation) and beat until they are just incorporated. Gradually pour in the hot milk, beating continuously. Return the mixture to the pan and bring it to a boil, stirring constantly with a whisk, reaching well into the corners. As soon as it reaches a boil, the mixture will become very thick. Boil gently for 1 minute, stirring constantly with the whisk. Remove the pan from the heat, whisk in the vanilla and pour the mixture into a bowl. Press a piece of plastic wrap directly onto the surface of the mixture to prevent a skin from forming, and allow it to cool at room temperature or refrigerate it. (You may speed it up by placing the bowl in the freezer for about half an hour, but do not use a metal bowl, and stir it 2 or 3 times.) When the *crème* is cool, whisk in the Grand Marnier until smooth, and set aside.

Whip the heavy cream until it is stiff (peaks will stand straight up when the beater is lifted) and fold it into the *crème*. Chill for at least 30 minutes or up to 3 days. Soften for piping, if necessary, in a *bain marie*, folding constantly. Fill the puffs only when you are ready to assemble the Gâteau. Use a Bismarck tube (long and narrow) and insert it into the slit in the bottom of the puff. Set the filled puffs aside and make the caramel.

To pipe: Fill the bag only half full so that the *crème* doesn't soften too quickly from the heat of your hand.

6¾ ounces (1 cup) sugar
⅓ cup water
⅛ teaspoon cream of tartar
(prevents crystallization)

CARAMEL

Combine these ingredients in a small heavy saucepan over medium-low heat and stir to dissolve the sugar. Increase the heat and boil without stirring until the mixture is amber in color (about 310 degrees). This will take about 8 minutes after boiling. Remove the pan from the heat and spoon a few drops of caramel onto the pastry round and affix the halo and curlicue. Allow the caramel to cool for 5 minutes to thicken for coating. Place the bottom of the pan in hot water or on very low heat to keep the caramel warm. If it hardens, it may be reheated briefly until the right consistency is reached.

Holding a puff at the bottom end with tongs, fingertips or a two-tined fork inserted in the side near the bottom, carefully dip the top into the caramel and allow the excess to drip onto the halo. Quickly attach the puff to the halo before the caramel hardens. Continue with the remaining puffs, working quickly until the circle of puffs is completed.

When cool, spoon a layer of Crème St. Honoré into the center. If desired, place a light layer of fruit on top. Fill the pastry bag with the remaining *crème* using a ¾-inch star or round tip, and pipe the *crème* decoratively on top. I like to make overlapping layers of the shell pattern. Set aside in a cool, dry area, or refrigerate.

NOTE: For optimum texture, the Gâteau should be completed the same day it is to be consumed. Prolonged chilling results in tough pastry, soggy puffs, sticky caramel and a skin on the *crème*.

SPUN SUGAR

This spun sugar is known as "angel's hair" and the ethereal, shimmering effect is well worth the effort.

3½ ounces (½ cup) sugar
⅓ cup corn syrup
1 teaspoon grated beeswax or paraffin (optional—beeswax is preferable because softer)

Cover the floor near the table or countertop with newspaper. Also tape newspaper to the edge of the counter to protect cabinets. Oil the handle of a long wooden spoon and tape the spoon to the countertop so that the handle extends beyond the edge.

Stir together the sugar and corn syrup in a small saucepan, and bring the mixture to a boil over medium heat. Increase the heat and boil until the liquid turns pale amber at about 335 degrees. Remove the saucepan from the heat and add the beeswax after cooling 2 to 3 minutes. If it is too hot it will fall in droplets instead of strings, it will not spin, and the wax will smoke.

Stand on a stool so that you are above the wooden handle. Hold 2 forks side by side in one hand. Dip them into the sugar and vigorously wave the forks back and forth above the handle, allowing the sugar to fall in long, thin threads. Waving must be continuous or droplets will form. It is normal to have a few small droplets, which are known as angel's tears.

Wrap the strands around the base and side of the Gâteau. Any leftover spun sugar may be stored for 2 to 3 weeks in an airtight container, if it is left in a cool dry area. It may also be frozen into little "nests" and filled with ice cream. These are best shaped immediately after spinning the sugar because the strands tend to become brittle and hard to shape. Do not even attempt to make spun sugar in hot and/or humid weather: it will collapse.

The optional wax coats the strands of spun sugar, making them easier to work with. It is also edible!

NOTE: To make ahead, use an oiled, inverted cake pan, the size of the finished cake, to wrap the spun sugar around. When the sugar hardens, carefully lift it off and wrap it well with plastic wrap or store it in an airtight container.

Gâteau à la Brioche

This unusual cake was inspired by Le Nôtre. In his week-long course for professionals, this cake was the most interesting. It is a study in contrasts—the gossamer-soft brioche saturated with a refreshingly light rum syrup and encased by an incredibly rich, light, smooth praline buttercream. This cake is refreshing yet quite sweet; the reason is both the praline buttercream and the 30 percent sugar syrup. This density of syrup is used frequently in European-style cakes because it keeps so very well. The cake will keep admirably refrigerated for a week and frozen for three months. If you plan to eat it within a few days, try reducing the sugar in the syrup to half a cup.

Round brioche layer, 1½ by 7 inches, trimmed of all crust (see below), or about 1 pound ready-made brioches, trimmed of crusts

14 ounces Special Rum Syrup (see Syrups, page 71)

½ recipe for Crème au Beurre Praliné (see page 76)

½ cup shelled, oven-toasted hazelnuts, peeled and coarsely chopped

About 16 whole oven-toasted hazelnuts, peeled, for decoration

BRIOCHE:

2½ tablespoons scalded milk cooled to warm (100 degrees if fresh yeast is used; 110 degrees if dry yeast)

2 packed teaspoons fresh compressed yeast or ½ package dry yeast

½ pound (1¾ cups) unbleached, all purpose flour (such as Heckers)

3 eggs, 1 at room temperature and 2 cold

1¼ ounces (3 tablespoons) sugar

¾ teaspoon salt

5 ounces (10 tablespoons) melted butter (not hot)

Making the Sponge:

If you are using fresh yeast, place it in the work bowl of a food processor with a metal blade, or preferably a special dough-kneading blade, and process it for a few seconds or until it is evenly crumbled. Add ⅓ cup of the flour and 1 egg. Process 2 to 3 seconds (10 if you are using the dough-kneading blade) and scrape down the sides of the bowl. Sprinkle the remaining flour over the mixture but do not mix it in. Cover and let it stand for 1½ to 2 hours.

Kneading the Dough:

Add the 3 tablespoons sugar, ¾ teaspoon salt and the 2 remaining (cold) eggs. Process for 15 seconds. With the machine on, pour in the melted butter in a steady stream. If the machine stalls, allow it to rest 3 minutes before continuing, and loosen the dough around the blade with a spatula. Process for 20 seconds longer. The batter will be a smooth cream.

First Rise:

Scrape this "cream" into a 3-quart bowl or pot. Sprinkle the top lightly with flour to prevent a crust from forming. Cover the bowl (airtight) with plastic wrap. Let the dough rise at room temperature until it is light, spongy and almost tripled in bulk. (Mark the side of the container with masking tape approximately where 3 times the bulk will come to.) This can take anywhere from 2 to 6 hours depending on the type of yeast and the temperature of the room. Using fresh yeast in a room at about 72 degrees, I find the first rising time is usually about 2¾ hours.

Deflating and Redistributing the Yeast Cells:

Deflate the dough by stirring it down, and refrigerate it for 1½ hours. Turn it onto a lightly floured surface and gently press it into a rectangle. Fold the dough into thirds (as in folding a business letter) and again press it out into a rectangle of the same size, lightly flouring the surface as needed to prevent stickiness. Fold it again into thirds and dust it lightly on all sides with flour. Wrap it loosely but securely in plastic wrap and then in foil and refrigerate it for 6 hours to overnight, to allow the dough to ripen and harden. The dough rises best if it has rested at least 24 hours, and you may keep it for up to 3 days. At this point you may either shape it or freeze it for future use, but this resting period is essential.

Shaping the Brioche:

Thoroughly butter, or spray with Pam, a 2-by-8-inch cake pan. Remove the dough from the refrigerator and press it firmly into the pan. Cover it loosely with buttered plastic wrap and allow it to rise in a warm humid area away from drafts for 2 to 3 hours or until the dough has doubled in bulk. (At 80 degrees it usually takes 2 hours, if you are using fresh yeast.)

Baking:

Preheat the oven to 425 degrees. Bake the brioche for 5 minutes, lower the temperature to 375 degrees and continue baking for 20 minutes or until a cake tester comes out clean. (Convection oven: 400 degrees for 5 minutes, 350 degrees for 10 minutes, 335 degrees for 10 minutes.) Unmold the brioche and cool it on a rack.

NOTE: To prepare the brioche dough in a heavy-duty electric mixer or by hand, use butter softened to room temperature instead of melted (it is easier to handle), and beat it in by the tablespoon. With the machine, change to a dough hook if the dough starts climbing up the sides of the spade beater. Beat for about 10 minutes on medium speed or until the dough is smooth and shiny. If kneading by hand, coat the flat of your hands well with flour as necessary to keep the dough from sticking, and beat from side to side without holding the dough or allowing it to rest in your hands. This is a sort of bouncing motion. If the dough sticks to the work surface, use a scraper to turn it over, then flour the counter and continue flouring your hands when necessary until the dough is smooth and glossy. Proceed as for the processor method. The 2 eggs are added cold to the dough to keep its temperature from getting too high. (This would result in a sour taste in the finished brioche.)

Composing the Cake:

To mold the cake, use either a 7½-inch cardboard round encircled with a 2-inch-high flan ring (preferably adjustable), or a 2-by-8-inch cake pan with a parchment or wax paper round on the bottom. Spread a small amount of praline buttercream on the cardboard and around the sides of the pan or flan ring to help slide the brioche in and to prevent the syrup from leaking.

Place the brioche in a different large pan and pour the syrup on top of it. Allow the brioche to sit for about 10 minutes, turning it occasionally to help it absorb the syrup. Place it

on a rack for 5 minutes to drain the excess syrup. The cake should have absorbed almost all the syrup (usually about 2 tablespoons remain).

Place the brioche in the prepared mold and top it with the buttercream. Use a long spatula to create a smooth top, allowing the spatula to rest on the sides of the mold. This creates a very even surface.

Chill the cake in the refrigerator for at least 2 hours. Run a small metal spatula around the sides of the mold and unmold it. With an expandable flan ring you have only to enlarge the sides and push the cardboard base up and out of the mold. With a cake pan, invert it onto a flat surface covered with plastic wrap and reinvert it immediately onto a 7½-inch cardboard circle.

Mask the sides of the cake with the praline buttercream and gently press the chopped nuts against the side. (See *Toppings*, Chopped Toasted Nuts, page 73.) Le Nôtre grates meringue on top. I sometimes dust it with pulverized caramel or pipe a border of stars alternating with whole toasted hazelnuts, which they resemble. Because of the mold, the cake should be absolutely symmetrical and therefore does not require any further enhancement.

It is best to allow cakes with syrup to mature at least 24 hours in the refrigerator, but it is fine to eat this cake right away. However, chill it at least until the buttercream firms slightly (5 minutes in the freezer or 30 minutes in the refrigerator).

Golden Heart Cake

Makes 12 servings

This is the richest and most subtly elegant of the non-chocolate cakes. It combines my favorite Génoise type of cake and buttercream. It is decorated simply with chopped toasted nuts, and powdered caramel, which sparkles like gold dust.

1 Golden Génoise recipe baked into heart shapes

½ recipe Crème au Beurre Praliné (see page 76)

½ cup shelled, oven-toasted hazelnuts, peeled and coarsely chopped

1 Caramel Powder recipe (see page 73)

Cut a heart-shaped cardboard base ½ inch larger than the cake and spread it with a little buttercream. Place one layer of heart-shaped cake on the cardboard. Spread it with buttercream and place the second layer on top. Frost it with buttercream.

Holding the cake in the palm of your hand, tilt it slightly and press the nuts onto the sides with a slightly cupped hand. Dust the top with caramel powder, using a small strainer. Refrigerate, but allow it to stand at room temperature for 30 minutes before serving.

Black Forest Cake *(Schwarzwälder Kirschtorte)* — *Makes 8-12 servings*

This is perhaps the most famous of German Konditorei desserts. My version uses a tart red cherry filling instead of the usual dark sweet cherries, and a cherry liqueur syrup instead of the usual eau de vie (Kirsch).

1 Chocolate Génoise recipe (Basic Chocolate Génoise or Moist Chocolate Génoise)

1 (7-ounce) Basic Syrup recipe (see page 71), using Cherry Heering or Cherry Marnier, only if using the Basic Chocolate Génoise recipe. For Moist Chocolate Génoise, use just a sprinkling of the liqueur alone

2 cups heavy cream, whipped with ¼ cup confectioners' sugar and ½ teaspoon almond extract

1 Tart Red Cherry Filling recipe (see page 72)

8-12 whole cherries

Semi-sweet chocolate curls (optional)

Trim the crusts and slice the Génoise into three ½- to ¾-inch layers. Brush all the sides with the syrup. Spread the cherry filling topped with whipped cream between the layers. Frost the cake with the whipped cream and decorate it with the whole cherries and chocolate curls.

Rhapsody Cake

In this recipe, I have combined several of the classic techniques of European pastry: the Génoise, sirop (syrup), meringue, crème au beurre mousseline (meringue buttercream) and crème chantilly (whipped cream). The basic ingredients are simply butter, cream, eggs, sugar and flour, yet each component of this cake has a unique character.

11-ounce can mandarin orange slices, well drained and marinated (preferably overnight) in 2 tablespoons Mandarine liqueur (see Syrup for Cakes, page 71)

1 Génoise recipe

1 Basic Syrup recipe (⅔ cup), using Mandarine liqueur

1 meringue recipe (see page 65)

1 Crème au Beurre Mousseline recipe (see page 75), using Mandarine liqueur

½ cup heavy cream, whipped with: 1 tablespoon confectioners' sugar ¼ teaspoon vanilla extract

Carefully trim the meringue discs to exactly 8 inches in diameter or the diameter of the Génoise. Drain the orange slices, reserving the liquid to add to the syrup. Dry the slices with paper towels. Trim the crusts from the Génoise and slice into two ¾-inch layers, reserving any remaining layers for a Grand Marnier soufflé or lining molds for a mousse. Brush each side of the layers with equal amounts of the syrup.

Spread a small amount of *mousseline* on an 8-inch cardboard round and attach 1 meringue disc. Spread a thin layer of *moussseline* on top of the meringue and place 1 layer of Génoise on top.

Spread the whipped cream on top of the Génoise and place about 14 orange slices on the whipped cream. Top with a second Génoise layer. Spread it with a thin layer of *mousseline* and top with the last meringue disc.

Frost the sides and top of the cake with the remaining *mousseline*, using the remaining orange slices as garnish for the top.

NOTE: The cake is best when it is allowed to ripen for 1 day in the refrigerator but will keep refrigerated for up to 5 days or frozen for up to 3 months. Allow it to stand at room temperature for 30 minutes before serving. In season, replace the orange slices with fresh raspberries or strawberries, and use Framboise liqueur for both the syrup and *mousseline*. If you are planning to do any elaborate decoration, increase the quantity of the *mousseline* slightly.

Meringue

The lightest and most delicate meringues are made with a combination of superfine and confectioners' sugar, never granulated sugar, which cannot dissolve into the egg whites no matter how long they are beaten, and results in meringues with the texture of cement.

> The classic proportion for meringue is double the weight in sugar for that of the egg white.
>
> 1 egg white measures 2 tablespoons (1 liquid ounce) and weighs 1 ounce
> 1 cup confectioners' sugar weighs 4 ounces
> 1 cup superfine sugar weighs 7 ounces

4 (4 ounces) egg whites (½ cup), at room temperature

4 ounces (9 tablespoons) superfine sugar

4 ounces (1 cup) confectioners' sugar, sifted

½ teaspoon cream of tartar (optional)

¼ teaspoon salt (optional)

Beat the whites with the salt on low speed until frothy. Add the cream of tartar, if desired, and raise the speed to medium. Continue beating while gradually adding 2 tablespoons of the superfine sugar. When soft peaks form, add another tablespoon of the superfine sugar and increase the speed to high. When stiff peaks form, gradually beat in the remaining superfine sugar. Fold in the confectioners' sugar and pipe or spread the mixture with a spatula onto a prepared cookie sheet.

NOTE: For chocolate meringue, sift 2 tablespoons of cocoa with the confectioners' sugar.

Baking:

Bake the meringues on a cookie sheet that is covered with a brown paper bag or parchment, or is teflon-coated.

Large shells or discs should bake at 200 degrees for 1½ hours, or until they are dry but not beginning to color. Ideally they should be baked for 1 hour and then be left overnight in a switched-off oven. They should actually be dried, not baked. Large, deep puffs may take up to 2 hours or more. Test for doneness by digging out a tiny piece from the bottom center with the tip of a sharp knife to be sure the meringue is no longer sticky inside.

Storage:

Tightly covered at room temperature and with low humidity, meringues will keep for up to 6 months. Ideal storage is in a cool, airy spot free from humidity—I have never found one.

Dacquoise

A dacquoise is a meringue made with the addition of ground nuts. A small amount of cornstarch is usually added to help absorb any grease exuded by the nuts, but it is important to grind the nuts in such a way that there is as little grease released as possible.

Dacquoises vary in the proportion of nuts and sugar to egg white, and some use nuts in quantities up to as much as two-thirds the combined weight of the egg whites and sugar. The proportions in the following recipe represent equal weights of nuts and egg whites and one and three-quarters their weight in sugar (instead of the double weight used in meringues). To my taste, these proportions result in the ideal texture and flavor.

4 ounces (¾ cup) peeled, finely ground almonds or hazelnuts
1½ tablespoons cornstarch
4 ounces (9 tablespoons) superfine sugar
3 ounces (¾ cup) confectioners' sugar, sifted
4 ounces (½ cup) egg whites, at room temperature
½ teaspoon cream of tartar (optional)
¼ teaspoon salt

Thoroughly combine the ground nuts, cornstarch, ½ cup of the superfine sugar and all the confectioners' sugar.

Beat the whites with the salt until frothy. Add the cream of tartar, if desired, and raise the speed to medium. Continue beating while gradually adding 1 tablespoon sugar. When soft peaks form, gradually add the remaining 2 tablespoons of sugar and beat until stiff peaks form. Fold in the nut mixture and bake and store as for meringue.

Uses:

These discs of meringue and *dacquoise* can be used as toppings (as in the Rhapsody Cake, which uses meringues as a component). They also make entrancing desserts on their own when filled with buttercream and dusted with confectioners' sugar or layered with whipped cream and various kinds of fruit. Australians know meringue discs topped with chopped fresh fruits and cream as Pavlovas. The classic French cake, Vacherin, is made from discs of *dacquoise* layered with *crème chantilly* and fresh raspberries.

Decorating and Care of the Completed Cake

If the cake is not level, use a serrated knife to level off the top.

TORTING

To cut a cake into thinner layers, place the cooled cake on a turntable and, using a very sharp, preferably serrated knife, cut out a groove, the thickness of the layer desired, all around the outside. This provides a track for the knife to "ride" in when cutting through the cake. Cut through the cake, using a firm forward and side-to-side motion. Check occasionally to be sure the knife is still in the groove. It is easiest to hold your hand palm downward on top of the cake while slicing it. This keeps your fingers safe when the knife slices through to the other side.

Smaller cake layers can be lifted off by hand, larger ones benefit from the support of a straight-edged cookie sheet or cardboard round.

SUPPORTING

Invert cake onto a serving plate or cardboard round. I prefer to use cardboard rounds, but if you are using a serving plate, place a few strips of wax paper under the cake to keep the platter clean. These are easy to slide out after the cake is iced. Cardboard rounds should be about ½ inch larger in diameter than the cake (¼ inch on all sides). This enables you to control the exact amount of frosting applied to the sides of the cake. I use only enough frosting to produce a smooth exterior: too much frosting is too rich to eat. Attach the cake to the cardboard with a dab of frosting.

COVERING THE CAKE

There are four basic methods of covering a cake:

1. Dusting with confectioners' sugar
2. Frosting and coating sides with roasted chopped nuts or using a decorating comb or fork to create grooves
3. Frosting and decorating with a pastry tube
4. Glazing (with or without buttercream underneath).

Frosting:

To frost a cake smoothly and evenly with buttercream usually takes practice. It is deceptive to look at cake-decorating books where you will see pictures of cakes with sides as smooth as plaster. Actually they *are* as close to plaster as you can get—they are invariably covered with royal icing (sometimes known as decorators' cement), which is allowed to dry very hard and then sanded down to a perfectly smooth finish, unobtainable with buttercream.

To frost the cake, use a metal spatula to cover the sides and top of the cake with a frosting of thin consistency. Heaping on large amounts will help to keep the crust from separating, and excess frosting is easy to remove.

There are two ways to smooth the top. One is by placing the cake on a turntable and holding a long spatula halfway across the cake with the blade flat against it. Pressing lightly, hold the spatula perfectly still and carefully turn the cake in a complete circle. The second way is to place the cake on the counter with two stacks of books of identical height on either side of the cake. The height of the books should be the finished height you want the cake to be—slightly lower than the top of the frosting heaped on the cake top. Using a long metal spatula or ruler, scrape across the top of the cake, allowing the spatula to rest on the books. This method is far more steady than trying to level by hand alone.

To smooth the sides, using a turntable, angle the spatula slightly and hold it in place against the side of the cake, turning the turntable in a complete circle. To do it by hand, hold the cake on your fingertips at face level and, using a small metal spatula, held at a slight angle opening toward you, start at the top of the cake and move the spatula counter-clockwise in short strokes, ending each stroke at the bottom of the cake. (This helps to prevent a lip of excess icing from forming at the top.) Rotate the cake in a clockwise direction by carefully walking your fingers. If the icing is difficult to smooth, dip the spatula in hot water, and be careful to shake off any excess water.

Glazing:
Glazing a cake can produce a shiny, flawless exterior that requires no further ornamentation. It is important that the consistency of the glaze be correct—too thick and it will not flow smoothly, too thin and it will not cover the cake well. To produce the proper consistency for a glaze, always test it when the temperature is tepid or just barely warm. A small amount

dropped from a spoon onto the glaze should rest on the surface for a few moments and then disappear completely and smoothly into the rest of the mass. If it remains on the surface, you will need to thin the glaze slightly. If it does not mound up at all, the glaze is probably too thin and more chocolate must be added.

If the glaze is the proper consistency but cools too much before pouring and lumps on the cake, there is a technique that will rescue it provided there is no buttercream beneath the glaze. Place the glazed cake in a very low oven (150 degrees) for just a few seconds, until the glaze has melted just enough to smoothen out.

To prepare a cake for glazing, brush all crumbs from its surface and place it on a cardboard cake round and then on a rack which is resting on a cookie sheet. Or you may ice the cake smoothly with Ganache or buttercream and chill it until it is very firm before glazing. This provides a lovely contrast.

It is strongly advisable to have more than enough glaze to cover the cake with one application: "touch-ups" never produce as smooth a covering.

Pour barely tepid glaze generously on top of the cake in the center, allowing excess to flow down the sides. To produce a thinner coating, use a large metal spatula, moving it back and forth to smooth the glaze on top. If any spots on the side remain uncovered, use a small metal spatula to lift up some glaze which has fallen onto the cookie sheet and apply it to the uncovered area. Lift up the rack and tap it lightly to settle the glaze. Then allow the glaze to set undisturbed. When it is set, lift the cake from the rack with a broad spatula or pancake turner. Remaining glaze can be frozen and reheated for subsequent use. For a second coat wait until the first coat is "tacky."

NOTE: When making a glaze, be sure not to mix it too vigorously, or bubbles will form and mar the smoothness of the finish. If this should happen, tap the bowl containing the glaze on the counter until all the bubbles are released and/or stir gently in a figure-of-eight motion. If a few bubbles appear in the finished glaze on the cake, prick them with a pin before the glaze sets.

STORING AND TRANSPORTING THE CAKE

A cake frosted and decorated with buttercream can be made a day ahead and left at room temperature. It will stay fresh for about 5 to 6 days in the refrigerator. Once cut into, be sure to cover the cut edges either with clinging plastic wrap or two slices of fresh bread attached with toothpicks. To transport a frosted cake and prevent smudging, attach it to a cardboard circle larger than the diameter of the finished cake. This will keep the sides of the iced cake from touching the sides of the box and ruining the decorations. Carefully lower the cake into the cardboard box, preferably one not too much larger than the cake. Damp terry towels placed in the bottom of the car trunk help to keep the cake box from sliding. Always take along a pastry bag filled with a little icing to do any emergency repair on the cake's borders or to attach any flower that may have become dislodged in transit.

To freeze a frosted cake, place it, uncovered, in the freezer until the frosting is very firm and will not be damaged by wrapping. Wrap it first with plastic wrap, then with heavy-duty aluminum foil, trying to eliminate as much air space as possible. Cakes freeze well for several months—if you are planning to freeze the cake for a substantial amount of time, the more layers of wrapping the better. The most airtight wrap is known as the drugstore wrap. The item to be wrapped is placed in the center of the foil and the two long sides are brought together so that the edges meet and are then folded over together several times until they are close to the body of the item being wrapped. The short ends are then folded in the same manner. Delicate decorations can be further protected by placing the wrapped cake in the box.

To defrost: If the cake is not iced, remove it from the freezer and thaw without unwrapping it. If desired, the cake can be freshened after thawing by placing it in a 350-degree oven for about 10 minutes.

To defrost a frosted cake, unwrap it and place it in the refrigerator overnight. If the frosting is subjected to rapid extremes in temperature, it is likely to form condensation or beading.

Fresh Flowers and Other Decorations

Flowers make exquisite decorations for serving and no special device is needed to keep them fresh. Simply use a round pointed object to form a hole and insert the stem.

If you are decorating the cake a day ahead, it is wise to use tiny plastic vials available through florists or cake-decorating supply places. Some come equipped with tiny sponges that hold enough water to keep the flowers fresh without splashing the cake.

Silk leaves are often more attractive and realistic than piped icing leaves.

A broad band of ribbon surrounding a cake can provide a simple and elegant decorating effect.

There are also various edible toppings and sidings that produce added flavor, texture and an attractive appearance (see next section).

Syrups and Toppings

Syrup for Cakes

Génoise and brioche are like sponges, ready to absorb wonderful flavors. Moistening the layers of a Génoise with a small amount of syrup both gives it flavor and keeps its texture downy-soft and moist. The cake should be well moistened but not saturated and soggy. A brioche, on the other hand, can provide an unusual and refreshing dessert when saturated with syrup.

Cakes that are moistened with syrup improve after a 24-hour resting period to "mature" and absorb the moisture evenly. They also freeze beautifully.

I find that ⅔ cup of syrup is just right to moisten two ¾-inch Génoise layers. Adjust according to your own taste.

BASIC ⅔ CUP (5½ OUNCES) SYRUP

⅓ cup water
2¼ ounces (⅓ cup) sugar
2 tablespoons liqueur

BASIC 7-OUNCE SYRUP

½ cup water
3½ ounces (½ cup) sugar
3 tablespoons liqueur

SPECIAL 14-OUNCE (1¾ CUP) RUM SYRUP

1¼ cups water
5¼ ounces (¾ cup) sugar
¼ cup dark rum

The basic method for making a syrup is to combine the water and sugar in a small saucepan and bring it to a boil, stirring to dissolve the sugar. Then remove the pan from the heat and cool. Add liqueur and store tightly covered in the refrigerator for up to 5 weeks. To use, brush equal amounts of syrup on both sides of the decrusted cake layers.

SPECIAL 7-OUNCE GRAND MARNIER AND FRESH ORANGE-JUICE SYRUP

3½ ounces (½ cup) sugar
⅓ cup Grand Marnier
¼ cup orange juice

For this particular syrup, combine all ingredients and bring to just under the boiling point, stirring to dissolve the sugar.

Tart Red Cherry Topping and Filling

Makes about 2 cups

Red cherries provide both beautiful color and a foil to temper the sweetness of a cake. If you prefer a soft, slightly runny coating as opposed to one more jelled, use the smaller amount of cornstarch.

16-ounce can tart, red, pitted, water-packed cherries
3½ ounces (½ cup) sugar
1½-2 tablespoons cornstarch
⅛ teaspoon red food coloring (optional)
⅛ teaspoon almond extract

Drain the cherries well and reserve ⅔ cup juice. Place the sugar and cornstarch in a saucepan and stir in the cherry juice until smooth. Add the cherries and food coloring (optional) and continue stirring over moderate heat until thickened, clear and boiling. Simmer for 1 minute. The liquid should be thick enough to just barely be able to drop from the spoon. Remove the pan from the heat, add the almond extract and cool.

NOTE: If you are using fresh cherries you will need almost 2 cups of pitted tart ripe cherries and ⅔ cup juice (yielded from pitting) or juice with water added to equal ⅔ cup.

To make a 9-inch cherry pie, double the quantity of the filling, prepare as directed and pour it into an unbaked pie shell. Bake at 375 degrees for 40 minutes.

Caramel Powder

Powdered caramel came into existence one day in my class when a well-to-do lady bemoaned my throwing out a small sheet of leftover caramel. I ground it up instead in the food processor and discovered that it resembles gold dust and adds a subtle sparkle to a finished cake. It will eventually become dark golden when exposed to air or moisture. The darker the caramel, the more golden the powder, but be careful not to burn it.

Do not make caramel on a very humid day: it will be sticky and impossible to pulverize.

3½ ounces (½ cup) sugar
2 tablespoons water

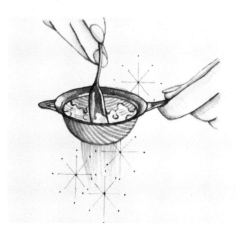

Combine the sugar and water in a small saucepan and cook over medium heat, stirring constantly until the sugar is dissolved. Raise the heat, and allow to boil undisturbed until the sugar begins to caramelize—it will look like dark corn syrup and smell like caramel.

Immediately pour the caramel onto a nonstick or greased baking sheet. Allow it to cool and harden, about 5 to 10 minutes. Lift it off the baking sheet by wedging your fingernail under the edge—it should come off easily. Break the caramel into pieces and grind them into a fine powder in small batches in a food processor or blender. Store the powder in an airtight jar at room temperature.

Chopped Toasted Nuts

Nuts surrounding a cake provide one of the easiest, most elegant and delicious decorative effects. Any leftover nuts will keep for months in the freezer and may be used as they are or recrisped in a 400-degree oven for 5 minutes. Almonds, hazelnuts, pecans and walnuts all make delicious coatings.

Remove the skin (see under *Ingredients*, Baking Soda) and place the nuts on a cookie sheet in a 350-degree oven for about 15 to 20 minutes or until they are lightly browned. Chop them coarsely. You will need about ½ cup or 2½ ounces of nuts to coat a 3-by-9-inch cake.

To apply: support the iced cake with a cardboard round in the palm of your hand. Tilt it a bit toward the other hand, which is slightly cupped to hold the nuts, and press the nuts gently into the side of the cake.

Meringue Mushrooms

These realistic little shapes make delightful decorations for the top of a cake or cake roll.

Use the Meringue recipe (page 65) or make a simpler, more sturdy meringue by beating in ¼ cup superfine sugar for each egg white. Pipe caps using the same technique as for pâte à chou. A large round tube is easier to use; approximately a half-inch opening is ideal (I often use the coupler). Hold the bag 90 degrees upright to the surface with the tube slightly above the parchment. Squeeze with a steady, even pressure, gradually raising the tube as the meringue begins to build up, but keeping the tip buried in the meringue. When you have achieved a well rounded shape, stop the pressure as you bring the tip to the surface. Use the tip to shave off any point, moving it clockwise. Points can also be removed by pressing gently with a moistened fingertip.

For the stems, use a #12 round tube and hold the bag perpendicular to the parchment with the tube touching it. Squeeze with heavy pressure, keeping the tip buried under the meringue until you build up a ¾-inch cone, wide enough at the base not to topple over.

Bake for about 45 minutes or until the mushrooms are firm enough to lift from the cookie sheet. With a sharp knife point, make a small hole in the underside of each cap. Pipe a tiny dab of leftover meringue into the hole and attach the stem, pointed end in. Place the mushrooms, cap down, on the cookie sheet and return them to the oven for about 20 minutes or until they are thoroughly dry.

If desired, dust the caps lightly with cocoa for an even more realistic effect. (I personally don't like to use chocolate because it looks less real than the rest of the mushroom.)

Frostings and Glazes

Crème au Beurre Mousseline *(Meringue Buttercream)*   *Makes 3½ cups*

This buttercream is silky-smooth, white and incredibly easy to work with—soft enough for beautiful shells and string work yet strong enough for side borders and even roses! It is, however, undeniably sweet, but the liqueur helps to temper it. One thing to watch for: if the room is hot or the butter too soft, what could have been a satin-smooth cream breaks down into a grainy, hopeless puddle. You can make this buttercream in the summer, but make sure the butter goes in still cold but just softened between your fingers.

3 egg whites
½ pound (2 cups) confectioners'
sugar
½ pound (16 tablespoons) butter,
softened but not warm
¼ cup liqueur such as Mandarine or
Grand Marnier

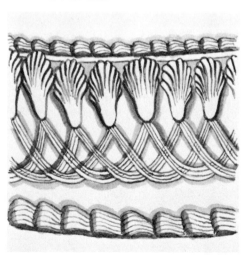

Place the egg whites and confectioners' sugar in the large bowl of an electric mixer. Set the bowl over a saucepan containing a few inches of simmering water, but do not allow the water to touch the bottom of the bowl. Stir the mixture with a whisk until it is creamy and no longer cold to the touch. The mixture must not begin to feel actually warm.

Remove the bowl from the saucepan and beat the mixture on high speed until it is very thick and glossy (about 5 minutes). The meringue will stand in almost stiff peaks. Cream the butter, and add it to the meringue by the tablespoon at medium-high speed.

When all the butter is incorporated, the mixture will still be stiff but less so than before. Gradually beat in the liqueur.

At first the mixture may seem to separate, but continue beating and it will magically smoothen and thicken into a luxurious cream. (This may take 2 or 3 minutes.) If the butter is too cold and forms lumps, allow the mixture to sit at room temperature until it softens, and then beat it until smooth. You may also beat it over hot water in a *bain marie*, but great care must be taken that it does not become too warm, and beating must be constant. For a chocolate *mousseline*, add 3 ounces of Tobler extra-bitter-sweet chocolate, and beat until it is incorporated.

Storage:
You may keep this buttercream at room temperature for several hours. For longer storage, refrigerate or freeze it, but be sure to allow it to come to room temperature before attempting to re-beat it, or it will break down irretrievably.

Crème au Beurre Praliné *(Praline Buttercream)* *Makes 4 cups*

This is my favorite—the one I long for when I fantasize about eating cakes. An incredibly rich and smooth buttercream, it is made with a base of super-rich crème anglaise—*almost as much egg yolk as milk. Butter enriches and thickens the cream, Italian meringue lightens it.*

Because of the small but necessary quantity of Italian meringue, this recipe cannot be cut to make less; however, any remainder may be kept for 10 days refrigerated, or frozen for up to six months without either flavor or texture being affected.

CRÈME ANGLAISE BASE:
½ cup milk
1¾ ounces (4 tablespoons) sugar
1¾ ounces (4 tablespoons) superfine sugar
5 egg yolks
½ teaspoon vanilla

ITALIAN MERINGUE:
3 ounces (7 tablespoons) sugar
2 tablespoons water
2 egg whites
Pinch of salt
14 ounces (28 tablespoons) butter, softened
4½ ounces (½ cup) Praline Paste (see *Ingredients*)

Crème Anglaise:
Bring the milk and the 4 tablespoons of sugar to a boil in a medium-sized heavy saucepan.

Whisk the yolks with the 4 tablespoons superfine sugar in a small bowl until well blended. Beat about 2 tablespoons of the hot milk mixture into the yolks, then add the yolks to the remaining mixture, whisking constantly. Bring to the boiling point, still whisking constantly, and sieve. If the mixture is not thoroughly smooth, beat it for about 2 minutes on high speed. When it is no longer hot, add the vanilla and cool.

Italian Meringue:
Stir together 6 of the 7 tablespoons of sugar and the 2 tablespoons of water in a small heavy saucepan. Heat, stirring constantly, until the sugar dissolves and the mixture is bubbling; stop stirring and continue cooking until a thermometer reaches 248-250 degrees (firm-ball stage).

While the syrup is boiling, start beating the egg whites with the pinch of salt until soft peaks form. Gradually add the sugar, beating until the peaks are almost stiff. When the sugar syrup reaches the correct temperature, beat it into the whites gradually, with the mixer on low. Continue beating, but raise the speed to medium-high until cool.

Cream the butter until it is soft. Add the *crème anglaise* base and beat on low speed until well blended. Using a rubber spatula, fold and stir in the meringue. If the mixture is very stiff, place the bowl over simmering water while stirring just for a few moments until the mixture softens enough to incorporate the meringue. Add the praline paste and stir briefly but vigorously until it is well blended.

NOTE: To make buttercream without praline, increase the sugar and superfine sugar to 6 tablespoons (2½ ounces) of each.

Cream Cheese Frosting

Makes 3 cups

This smooth, creamy, mellow, off-white frosting pipes and spreads with great ease. To pipe roses, more confectioners' sugar may be added for extra stiffness (be sure to sift it first) or chill the frosting until it is firmer.

8 ounces (16 tablespoons) butter softened to room temperature
8-ounce package cream cheese, softened
8 ounces (2 cups) confectioners' sugar
1 teaspoon vanilla extract or fresh lemon juice

Beat together the butter and cream cheese; add the remaining ingredients gradually, beating on low speed, and then raise the speed to high and continue beating until the frosting is smooth and fluffy.

To Pipe Roses:

Pipe each rose on a rose nail (these metal, large-headed nails are obtainable at bakers' supply stores) covered with wax paper. Place finished roses on a cookie sheet in the freezer until firm; store in a single layer in a freezer container; separate the layers with bubble wrap or several layers of plastic wrap. When you are ready to use the roses, place them directly on the cake. They keep indefinitely.

White Chocolate Cream Cheese Frosting

Makes 3 cups

For an interesting variation, try this frosting, which has both an unusually smooth texture and unusual, delicious flavor.

2 8-ounce packages cream cheese, softened

12 ounces white chocolate, melted (Lindt or Tobler)

1 teaspoon lemon extract (optional)

Beat the cream cheese on high speed until it is soft and fluffy. Add the melted chocolate and beat it in. Add the lemon extract if desired.

White Chocolate Frosting and Glaze

I am very excited about the creation of this unusual glaze and its properties as piping frosting. The glaze is satin-smooth, ivory and delicious. The white chocolate requires only a small amount of unflavored oil (mineral or vegetable) to soften it for easy slicing. The oil also contributes an added sheen to the glaze.

When the glaze mixture is allowed to harden, it becomes capable of piping the most exquisitely articulated shell border I have ever seen. Care must be taken to use small parchment bags and not to overfill them, because the heat of the hand quickly melts the chocolate and then it must be firmed up again before continuing. It's worth the effort, however, the effects are so breathtaking!

Strawberries dipped in the glaze are beautiful and the white chocolate does not overpower their flavor as does the dark chocolate.

To Make Glaze:

You will need 21 ounces of white chocolate to glaze a 3-by-9-inch cake. This may seem excessive, but you have to have enough to glaze the cake all at once so you do not need to "patch." If any spots remain uncovered, quickly use a metal spatula to lift the glaze and cover them before it starts to set. There will be a substantial amount of glaze left over, which may be stored and reused later.

Melt the chocolate and stir in the mineral oil (use 1 teaspoon oil for each ounce of chocolate). Stir with a whisk over ice water or allow it to sit until it mounds just a tiny bit when dropped from the spatula before disappearing into the mixture. For piping, continue chilling or allow the glaze to set until it starts to firm but does not peak. If it gets too stiff, it can be rewarmed slightly, stirring constantly with the whisk. It must be soft enough to flow when put into the bag. If you are stirring over ice water, be very careful not to allow even one drop of water to enter the chocolate or it will stiffen irrevocably.

To glaze a dark chocolate cake some people like to frost the sides first with buttercream or slightly chilled white chocolate glaze, or to give the whole cake two coats (let the first one set before reglazing, though). The object of this is to prevent the darkness from showing through. It is not absolutely necessary—indeed, I prefer the slightly darker stippled texture of the cake showing through the glaze.

Dark Chocolate Glaze

Use the same technique as for the White Chocolate Glaze. You may, however, add up to 2 teaspoons of oil per ounce of chocolate, because the dark chocolate is somewhat firmer.

Ganache

Once you have made the acquaintance of "Swiss Ganache" you will never be long without it—there is nothing quite like Ganache for filling, frosting, glazing or even saucing. Best of all, it can be frozen for periods up to several months without losing its quality.

This Light Ganache is wonderfully smooth and rich, though not as heavy as a buttercream. It can even be used for piping. For best texture and results it should be used shortly after preparing. If used as a filling or frosting, it may remain at room temperature for several hours.

The basic formula for Light Ganache is ¼ cup heavy cream for each ounce of chocolate. I use extra-bitter-sweet, but semi-sweet is fine as well.

Basic Recipe for Light Ganache
Makes about 2½ cups

1 cup heavy cream
4 ounces Tobler extra-bitter-sweet chocolate (or 3 ounces semi-sweet and 1 ounce unsweetened), chopped
1 tablespoon vanilla-flavored Cognac (see *Ingredients*, Vanilla) (optional)

Method One:
The easiest way to make Ganache filling is with the food processor. (No need to chop the chocolate first.) Process the chocolate until it is in very fine particles. Heat the cream to the boiling point and, with the motor running, pour it through the feed tube in a steady stream. Process until smooth.

Method Two:
Heat the cream and chocolate in a small heavy saucepan or the top of a double boiler over simmering water, stirring, until the chocolate melts and the mixture is very smooth and uniform in color. If tiny bits of chocolate remain, allow the mixture to sit in the pan for about 20 minutes, stirring occasionally, and the residual heat will dissolve them.

Pour the mixture into the large bowl of an electric mixer and refrigerate it until cold, stirring once or twice. This usually takes about 1½ hours. If the mixture is beaten when it is too cold, it will develop a grainy texture.

You can start beating with the electric mixer, but as soon as the mixture begins to thicken you should change to a hand whisk: it is very easy to overbeat. Overbeating causes the

Ganache to break down and separate. If this should happen, it can be rescued by re-melting, re-chilling and reheating. Add the Cognac, if desired, and beat only until soft peaks form.

Heavier Ganache or Ganache Glaze
Makes about 1 cup

½ cup heavy cream
4 ounces Tobler extra-bitter-sweet
  chocolate, chopped
1 tablespoon vanilla-flavored
  Cognac
4 teaspoons butter, softened

This formula uses half the amount of heavy cream in proportion to the lighter Ganache—2 tablespoons (1 ounce) heavy cream for each ounce of chocolate. Prepare as for Light Ganache, but allow to cool at room temperature. When cool add 1 teaspoon of softened butter for each ounce of chocolate. (This helps it to beat to a better volume.) For a wonderfully fudgy effect, chill until the ganache is firm enough to spread without whipping.

Ganache also makes the most delicious chocolate glaze. Use the recipe for the Heavier Ganache, omitting the butter. Approximately two cups will amply glaze a 3-by-9-inch cake, with plenty left over. Do not use the food processor, because it would cause air bubbles to appear in the glaze. Allow it to cool slightly before adding the Cognac. Start with 2 teaspoons of Cognac and, if the glaze seems too thick when tepid, add enough more Cognac that a small amount of glaze dropped from a spoon will mound up on the surface for a moment before disappearing smoothly into the glaze.

GANACHE ROSES

3 ounces Tobler extra-bitter-sweet
  chocolate, tempered
4 tablespoons heavy cream at room
  temperature
1 tablespoon confectioners' sugar

Stir together the cream and sugar to dissolve the sugar, and stir the mixture into the chocolate. Allow the mixture to set at room temperature or chill over ice water, stirring constantly with a whisk. Fill a pastry bag and pipe.

CHOCOLATE TRUFFLES

Chocolate truffles are delicious to serve by themselves, and make attractive decorations heaped in the center of a chocolate-glazed cake. The centers are made with the stiffer version of Ganache. Whenever I have any Ganache left over from a filling or glaze, I always turn it into truffles.

Chill the Ganache for a short time, until it is stiff enough to pipe from a pastry bag or to scoop with a small melon-baller. Pipe or scoop small mounds, no larger than ¾ inch, onto a cookie sheet and chill or freeze until firm. Dip in tempered chocolate, and when set, roll in cocoa. (Or they can be merely rolled in cocoa without being dipped into tempered chocolate.)

If you like the contrast of a bitter exterior, use plain cocoa. If you prefer a slightly sweeter result, use 1 part confectioners' sugar to 3 parts cocoa.

To create the rough-hewn texture of a true truffle, roll the cocoa-coated truffles lightly over a piece of screen or a sieve.

Refrigerated, chocolate truffles will keep about 3 weeks; frozen, they will keep for several months.

Chocolate Decorations

CIGARS

Long, tight spirals of chocolate are made by spreading melted chocolate in a thin layer about ⅛ inch thick on a smooth marble or formica counter. As soon as the chocolate has set enough, start making the cigars, because as the chocolate hardens it will become too brittle to work with. Tempering helps to control the chocolate but is not absolutely necessary.

To form cigars, use a long, very sharp knife held at a slight angle. The blade should be facing to your right. Start at the upper edge of the chocolate, bushing the knife firmly against the counter toward your right and at the same time pulling the knife toward you. This will cause the chocolate to roll. For thicker, looser cigars, spread the chocolate more thickly.

CURLS

Small chocolate curls are easiest to make using a block of chocolate and a vegetable peeler. To make a chocolate block, line a small Pyrex cup or ice-cube container with aluminum foil and pour in the melted chocolate. When fully set, remove and peel off the foil.

If the chocolate is too cold and hard, the curls will crack; if too warm and soft, they will be very tightly curled. I usually leave the chocolate block in the kitchen for a few hours at about 80 degrees. This seems to be just the right consistency to work with.

To keep the chocolate from melting in your fingers, hold the block with a piece of paper towel.

CUTOUTS

Sheets of chocolate can be cut into many shapes to be used as cake decorations. It is best to temper the chocolate to prevent a grayish bloom from forming. Spread the chocolate ⅛ inch thick on wax paper. When it has set enough to cut, use either a cookie cutter or a template and the sharp point of a knife to create shapes. Do not wait until the chocolate becomes very hard or the shapes may crack.

Use a small metal spatula to slide between the wax paper and chocolate decoration and carefully lift it off.

ROSE LEAVES

Chocolate rose leaves are exquisitely realistic. When used with a chocolate rose, the entire flower looks as if it were a real one dipped into chocolate to preserve it. It is best to temper the chocolate or to use compound chocolate to avoid the bloom. Use well-shaped (real) rose leaves with no holes. Spraying the leaves with nonstick vegetable shortening helps to release them from the chocolate but is not absolutely necessary. Hold the leaf by the stem, supported underneath by a finger.

With a small metal spatula, carefully paint the melted chocolate onto the underside of the leaf, being careful not to allow the chocolate to get on the other side of the leaf for ease in removal. (A paint brush would seem to be the ideal tool,

but it is not!) If the chocolate seems thin, allow it to set and apply a second coat.

Place the coated leaf on a cookie sheet, or preferably a flower former, which is curved and gives the leaves a more realistic shape. When set, peel off the leaf.

CHOCOLATE WRITING

To use chocolate for writing messages on cakes or fine-lined free-form designs, add a few drops of glycerine to the melted chocolate to thicken it very slightly. Pour into a parchment bag and cut off a tiny bit of the tip. Allow the chocolate to fall from the tip in a thin, flowing line, using the motion of your entire arm to form shapes. This produces a very elegant script and decoration.

Truffle Cups

Makes 18 1-inch bonbon foil cups

If I were serving a formal dinner with many courses and wanted a tiny, not-too-filling, but exquisitely satisfying dessert I would serve two of these truffle cups per person.

2 ounces Tobler extra-bitter-sweet chocolate, tempered
2 ounces Tobler bitter-sweet chocolate or extra-bitter-sweet
¼ cup heavy cream
1 teaspoon butter
2 teaspoons liqueur, preferably Frangelico or Kahlua
1 tablespoon Praline Paste (optional)

Temper the 2 ounces of extra-bitter-sweet chocolate and, using a small paint brush, coat the inside of the bonbon cups. Allow to set at room temperature or chill in the refrigerator.

Melt the other 2 ounces of chocolate in a small heavy saucepan or the top of a double boiler over hot water. Gradually stir in the heavy cream, then the butter, stirring until smooth. Remove the pan from the heat and stir in the liqueur. Allow the mixture to cool completely, then spoon or pipe it into the chocolate-lined bonbon cups. Chill or freeze them until they are firm. Serve in the foil cups or carefully peel away the foil and spread in a circle like a halo around the truffle. They are best eaten when chilled.

NOTE: I prefer the extra-bitter-sweet for the inside, but if you like your candies a little on the sweet side, use the bitter-sweet. It is important to use the extra-bitter-sweet for the outside of the cup, because it is darker and glossier. Alternatively, white chocolate used for the outside layer of the cups makes a stunning contrast. (Two coats are necessary.)

Refrigerated, these cups keep for 3 weeks, frozen for several months.